YEADON'S REGISTER

of

L N E R

LOCOMOTIVES

Volume Twenty- Nine

**Class D5, D6, D7, D8, D9, D10, D11/1 & D12
the Great Central 4-4-0's**

Copyright Book Law Publications 2003
ISBN 1 899624 63 5

YEADON'S REGISTER OF L.N.E.R. LOCOMOTIVES - VOLUME 29

EDITOR'S NOTE & ACKNOWLEDGEMENTS

This volume of the *Register* covers the 4-4-0 tender engines of the Great Central Railway, classes D5 to D12 but not including the D11/2. Already we have covered the Great Eastern and Great Northern engines of the same wheel arrangement but there are still those inherited from the North Eastern and North British companies to cover. It is within the volume spotlighting the NBR 4-4-0's where the D11/2's will find a home.

Perhaps some of you will be disappointed that the D11/2's have not been included within this particular volume where, some of you may say, they rightly belong but due to space considerations and the vast photographic coverage of the Scottish 'Directors', it was deemed impossible to include them here. However, seeing as the D11/2's spent their working lives north of the border, it is not inappropriate that they should be in the same volume as the other Scottish 4-4-0 tender engines.

Once again Eric Fry has sorted through the mountain of numbers, facts and illustrations to make sure that all is as it should be - thank you Eric.

Thanks also to Mike and Tina for the continuing slog of typesetting which, in this case, is no mean feat. Andy, David, Richard and Robert are just a few of the wizards at Amadeus Press who continually turn out a superb finished product.

By the time that this volume is published, a new Archivist would have taken the helm at the University of Hull but special thanks must go to Helen Roberts who has looked after the Archive in the absence the retiring Brian Dyson.

Although Jean and Simon live in Canada, they make regular visits to the UK to make sure that everything connected with this series is properly conducted and their enthusiasm is unabated.

The next *Yeadon's Register of LNER Locomotives*, Volume 30, contains the repair history of the locomotives with the 2-4-0 wheel arrangement classified within the E group.

Amendment to Volume 28. Normally within each volume of the *Register* the odd numerical or grammatical mistake might appear and, even though every care is taken to avoid them, we hold our hands up to their existence. Sometimes we get a letter or two from eagle-eyed readers who have spotted such a (trivial) mistake but these letters simply point out the error and then go on to wish us well with the remaining volumes in the series. However, in Volume 28 the gremlins had a 'field day' with three howlers for which we can only apologise and promise not to do it again! Our benefactor would have been none too pleased either but would have been forgiving knowing that nobody is infallible. Anyway, to put the record straight, the top illustrations on pages 2 and 6 have been transposed - the long tank version of No.116 should have appeared first. The photograph at the top of page 25 features a real cuckoo-in-the-nest. Not content with appearing in larger format on page 78, the WM&CQ tank nudged out R1 No.3121. Sorry.

> *The Yeadon Collection is available for inspection and anyone who wishes to*
> *inspect it should contact:-*
> The Archivist
> Brynmor Jones Library
> University of Hull
> Hull
> HU6 7RX
> Tel: 01482-465265
> A catalogue of the Yeadon collection is available.

First published in the United Kingdom by
BOOK LAW PUBLICATIONS 2003 in association with CHALLENGER
382 Carlton Hill, Nottingham, NG4 1JA.
Printed and bound by The Amadeus Press, Cleckheaton, West Yorkshire.

INTRODUCTION

The eight classes of locomotive featured in this volume all had their origins on one railway - the Great Central. The featured classes - D5, D6, D7, D8, D9, D10, D11/1 and D12 - consisted amongst their number some of the ablest and probably the most elegant 4-4-0 types in the country.

D5

Six engines, Nos.694 to 699 were built in 1895 by the Manchester, Sheffield & Lincolnshire Railway at Gorton, becoming Class 11 and later LNER D5. Although built two years into the regime of Harry Pollitt, the then MS&L Locomotive Superintendent, the design was based somewhat on his predecessor's Class 2A design (LNER D7). However, this class became the first MS&L passenger tender locomotives to have Belpaire fireboxes from new.

Unsuperheated at first, only two members of the class were to get superheated boilers, albeit rather late in their lifetimes, No.5694 in November 1925 and No.5695 in August 1926. When their original boilers were replaced between 1906 and 1916 with the GC Standard No.3 boiler, some of the last engines to get the No.3 boiler had the safety valves fitted directly onto the firebox. From 1911 extended smokeboxes were fitted although the last ones to get these, Nos.695 and 699, did not receive them till about 1918. All had Ramsbottom safety valves, but two engines received boilers with 'pop' valves late in life. These boilers were secondhand from D6 engines and were fitted to No.5698 in December 1926 and No.5696 in November 1927.

Two of the class, 5694 and 5699 lost their original Robinson chimneys which were replaced by the 'plantpot' type in November 1925. The former engine receiving its 'plantpot' at the same time as a superheated boiler.

For possible work on the London Extension, of which the class as a whole did very little, all six engines gained 4000 gallon tenders which replaced the original 3080 gallon type. However, by Grouping all except 698 and 699 had reverted to the smaller tender which was to change again when it was realised that the 4000 gallon type was much more useful with these engines. The tenders came from J10 class goods engines and by November 1927 all had the larger tender coupled once again.

LNER passenger green livery had been applied to all engines by the end of 1924 and three engines got the C suffix in 1923. The 1928 painting economies saw five engines having black with single red lining applied; No.5696 managed to keep its green livery until withdrawal in July 1930.

Built for working the principal London express passenger trains of the time between Manchester and Grantham, these engines were employed for only a couple of years on these jobs being superseded by thirty-odd Class 11A (LNER D6) built from 1897 onwards (see later). However, they continued to work between Sheffield and Grantham during the first years of the 20th century with through coaches to King's Cross. From new the whole class was allocated to Gorton but as the 11A's took over the more important passenger duties, now via the Extension, they were relegated to secondary duties and within ten years all six had ended up at Neepsend shed in Sheffield. From there they worked east to the Lincolnshire coast and south as far as Leicester, work which they continued to do virtually up to Grouping. Although of slight stature compared with later built 4-4-0's (D9,

D10 for instance) the D5's were very capable locomotives and during their period on 'secondary' duties they could often be found hauling ten or more coaches, especially during the Great War years.

Just before the Grouping all six D5's were sent to work on the Cheshire Lines being shedded first at Trafford Park where they worked mainly to Chester but occasionally to Liverpool. The whole class were allocated to Walton-on-the-Hill during the mid-1920's from where they were sub-shedded to Southport on duties which would not tax their capabilities but in 1928 they all returned to Trafford Park where they took on mundane 'local' workings. This was then their lot during the final years of their lives. In July 1930 the first withdrawal took place when No.5696 was condemned; the last to go was 5699 in March 1933.

D6

Between September 1897 and April 1899 thirty-three 4-4-0 express passenger engines were introduced onto the Great Central ready for the opening of the London Extension and the company's accelerated services from Manchester to London. The design was yet another 'improvement' by Pollitt on the Parker design of Class D7, the most important being the provision of piston valves to the cylinders.

The new engines were built by both the company's own workshops at Gorton and the neighbouring locomotive builder Beyer, Peacock & Co. Nos.268, 269, 270 and 852 to 861 were built at Gorton and Nos.862 to 881 at Beyer, Peacock, their works numbers being 3980 to 3999. It is still not clear exactly which of the engines purportedly built at the latter establishment were actually constructed there because during the period of building, Beyer, Peacock had an industrial dispute on its hands. Gorton being somewhat desperate for the new engines apparently agreed to build some of Beyer, Peacock's order in the railway's own workshops which seems to have been the case, but during the construction period the Beyer, Peacock strike was settled and the work in hand at Gorton was sent across to Gorton Foundry - as the BP works were known locally - for finishing just in time to start work on the Extension.

Saturated boilers were fitted to these engines from new and it was to be the second decade of the 1900's before superheating started. Five of the class had not received superheaters by Grouping, and No.871c reverted to saturated in December 1923. It again received a superheated boiler in August 1925 and it took until as late as 1934 before the entire class became superheated, nearly four years after the first withdrawals had taken place.

Until November 1924 all the class were well over the 13ft 0in. composite load gauge. The Robinson chimney being 13ft 2³/4in. and the height over dome stud 13ft 3¹/4in. from rail level. In November 1924 No.5859 got a new boiler as did No.5855 in February 1925, and these two changed to the 'plantpot' chimney which cut height from rail to 12ft 10³/4in. A shorter dome reduced that height to 12ft 8¹/2in. All the class changed to the 'plantpot' chimney although ten were withdrawn without having a new lower dome and therefore were never within the Composite Load Gauge.

Six engines Nos.694 to 699 were built at Gorton in 1895. No.695 is shown as fitted with Robinson chimney, short smokebox, Ramsbottom safety valves, three washout plugs, 3080 gallon tender, and with ash ejector to smokebox.

The thirty-three engines in Class D6 were built in 1897-99, all with a short cab roof. This was extended from 1912 onwards to finish level with the cab side sheet. Note taper shank buffers and 3080 gallon tender coupled.

Ash ejectors were introduced to the D6 class from 1911 and all the class were so fitted though the steam supply pipe varied in length depending on different periods of fitting or if fitted to saturated or superheated type boiler and modification. Normally the steam pipe was on the left side of the smokebox but on those which had Westinghouse pump the pipe was fitted on the right side. In the middle 1930's No.5853 had its ash ejector removed but this was only temporary as it was refitted at a general repair in January 1938.

In 1902/3 four, Nos.857, 859, 869 and 876, were fitted with additional Westinghouse brake to work stock from the Great Eastern, mainly the Harwich-Liverpool boat trains. They were still on this work to 1927 when B12 and (later) B17's took over. From 1927 the need for Westinghouse equipment diminished but No.5857 kept it to withdrawal in August 1931. It was taken off 5859 in the May and 5876 in the October of 1932. The removal was completed when No.5869 was shopped in January 1934. Once the Westinghouse gear was taken off the ash ejector steam pipe was moved to the normal position on the left side of the smokebox.

At introduction this class were spread out between Gorton, Neepsend, Leicester, Woodford and Neasden sheds working the principal expresses on the new main line, but from 1902 the Robinson 4-4-0's of LNER Class D9 began to share and then monopolise this work and eventually the majority of the D6's ended up on the Cheshire Lines shared between Trafford Park and Brunswick. Only the four Westinghouse engines had not been sent to Lancashire, these had settled at Lincoln for working the boat trains off the GER.

Whilst on the Cheshire Lines the D6 engines worked the Liverpool-Hull expresses with at least one engine permanently stationed at Hull Dairycoates to balance the workings of these trains.

Except for a few inevitable wartime changes during the 1914-18 conflict, the class remained virtually as they had in 1909 although Lincoln's four were now shared between Mexborough and Retford. Just before Grouping the whole class was reassembled in Lancashire at Brunswick and Trafford Park purely to work the principal CLC trains between Manchester and Liverpool. Even the Westinghouse engines ended up there with two at each shed for working the Manchester-Liverpool leg of the Harwich boat train.

In the late 1920's a few of the class shuffled between Walton-on-the-Hill, Southport and Brunswick. Heaton Mersey got a couple for stopping passenger services to Liverpool and even St Helens. In 1937 two D6's moved to Immingham in place of D7's; two more went to that depot before the outbreak of WW2 but they then went to Brunswick during the early war years. In 1941 Chester and Northwich sheds gained two each but three of those returned to Lancashire in the following year and only No.5859 remained at Northwich. This engine was withdrawn in 1945 and the three remaining D6's took its place at Northwich in 1946.

No.5874 was the last to have a general repair, ex works 24th August 1946. Whilst at Gorton 'Tank' for this last repair, the ash ejector was removed; it also had the wheel of the smokebox door fastening changed for another handle. Its renumbering to 2106 did not occur until 3rd November 1946.

Only two other D6's actually gained their 1946 numbers; 2101 (ex5855) in May 1946, and 2104 (ex5865) in December 1946.

The first two D6's were condemned in 1930, No.5873 in June and No.5866 in September, with six more going the following year. In 1932 four more succumbed whilst 1933 also

saw four withdrawn, the last until November 1935 when only No.5875 was withdrawn. Seven more of the class were condemned before the outbreak of war whilst the nine survivors nearly all worked through the war years; only Nos.5869 and 5879 being withdrawn during this period. Eight of the wartime engines were allocated new numbers in the 1943 scheme (5869 was withdrawn in June 1943 so did not qualify) but as mentioned above only three actually received them.

Like so many other ex GC engines, the last D6, No.2106 (5874) was condemned on the very last day of the LNER. The D6 class as a whole had put in a creditable performance and no doubt wartime had lengthened their working lives, No.2106 had put in nearly fifty years service at its demise.

D7

Thirty-one engines made up this MS&LR class, the first of which appeared in 1887. Built by Kitson & Co., MS&L No.561 was the first single framed engine on the railway. This departure from the normal double-framed company practice was probably down to the maker's who had, it is believed, quite a say in its design.

The engine became MS&L Class 2 and was the only one of its kind on the railway until Parker added six more Gorton built examples in 1890, numbered 562 to 567. These six had somewhat deeper frames than No.561, a change no doubt brought about from operational experience with the original design. During 1891 and 1892 the class was expanded by the addition of six Gorton built examples and a dozen more from Kitson's. Finally in 1894 Parker had six more built by Gorton but these differed from the other twenty-five in having coiled as against leaf springs and larger wheel journals. The last six engines became Class 2A because of these minor differences.

From 1901 Robinson fitted seven of the class with new longer smokeboxes and his own brand of chimney but between 1909 and 1918 all of the class were fitted with Belpaire boilers and the original stovepipe chimney retained by the rest of the class was also changed to the Robinson type. In 1912 a start was made to extend the cab roof towards the back and this was completed by the time the boilers had all been changed to Belpaire. During the early years of the LNER period flowerpot chimneys replaced the Robinson type and most of the class received these.

Two of the class, Nos.700 and 705, were fitted with Westinghouse brakes from 1903 to enable them to work stock from the GER and NER when necessary. All the rest kept to the vacuum brake only for both engine and train. The Westinghouse engines kept that equipment until the early 1930's, No.5705 up to withdrawal.

Allocated at first to work the Manchester - London expresses to and from Grantham, and other important express trains, these 4-4-0's were in turn relegated from those duties by more modern engines and by 1900 were mainly used for secondary work, Sheffield Neepsend shed having a large allocation of them until about 1918 then, just a few years before Grouping, nearly two-thirds of the class migrated to Lincolnshire with ten each at Immingham and Lincoln sheds in 1921. The others, except for four at Northwich, stayed east of the Pennines at Mexborough and Retford. After Grouping most of the class ended up in England's second largest county and besides Immingham and Lincoln housing the D7's, Frodingham, Louth and New Holland also had use for them. Mexborough kept three until the mid 1930's but these ended their days too in Lincolnshire.

From June 1928, D7 class no longer qualified for green paint, but four, Nos.5561, 5563, 5564 and 5693 carried it to withdrawal. All the rest changed to black paint with single red lining.

Withdrawal generally did not start until October 1929 but No.5564 was condemned in December 1926 and No.5561 in September 1928. It is fairly certain that only these two were never fitted with the 'plantpot' chimney.

The last two D7's survived to 1939, Nos.5684 and 5704 being the sole members of the class since mid-1937.

D8

Only three of this class (GCR Class 6DB) were built, all in 1888, and at Gorton. Originally numbered 37, 89 and 400 by the MS&L, the engines had been renumbered 508, 510 and 511 respectively in 1893, and had reached Grouping as part of the Great Central Duplicate List fleet. To allow their numbers to be used by the 'Improved Directors', Nos.508 and 510 were given the B suffix in 1920 and No.511 got it in 1922.

These double framed 4-4-0's were a Parker development of an earlier Sacré 2-4-0 design and had worked the important Manchester - London express's for the first five years of their lives, sharing those duties with the Parker Class 2 4-4-0's (LNER Class D7), a class which eventually ousted them from those workings. In 1893 all three were sent to Brunswick shed to work the Liverpool - Hull passenger trains which they continued to do for about another six years when they were then relieved from that job by younger, more able classes.

Vacuum brakes were fitted as standard to all three engines.

About 1900 Robinson fitted new smokeboxes and his own design of chimney, then in 1910/12 replaced the round-top firebox boilers with his Standard No.1 Belpaire type. The cab roofs were also extended so as to shelter the whole footplate.

For virtually the rest of the GC period these three engines performed most of their duties, which were now of a secondary nature, in Lincolnshire with Lincoln and New Holland sheds using them accordingly. Just before Grouping they moved back to Lancashire, taking up residence in Southport like so many other 'pensioners'. From the seaside town they worked out their remaining years on passenger trains to both Liverpool and Manchester.

Only one of the trio got an LNER number; No.510B became 6415 in December 1924. The other two had been scrapped before they were even allocated a number under the LNER scheme. No.6415 itself was withdrawn in March 1926, its singleton non-standard status rendering it redundant.

D9

The forty engines which comprised LNER Class D9 was J.G.Robinson's first express passenger engine type built for the Great Central. All were built by outside contractors; Nos.1013 to 1042 by Sharp Stewart & Co. during 1901, 1902 and 1903, with Vulcan Foundry supplying the last ten, Nos.104 to 113 in 1904. The design was essentially an enlargement of Parker's Class 11 (LNER D5) 4-4-0 and reverted to the use of slide valves in place of the piston type that had been introduced two years later by Pollitt on his 11A (LNER D6) engines.

On the GCR, the engines were subject to rebuilding from early on due to their somewhat poor performance and eventually the class fell into three sub classes, Class 11B, 11C and 11D. 11B class was the original design, with 18$^1/_2$ in. diameter cylinders using saturated steam; 11C had a bigger boiler, both in diameter and length of firebox, and with cylinders enlarged to 19in., and 11D was the final version in which the firebox length reverted to the original figure and new cylinders with piston valves were provided. The initial conversion had a saturated boiler bur superheating was standard thereafter.

The early efforts to improve this class by reboilering and fitting new cylinders with piston valves was rather complex and the sequence of events can be summarised as follows:
1. The original design had a 4ft 9in. diameter boiler with Belpaire firebox using saturated steam. Cylinders were 18$^1/_2$ in. diameter and had slide valves.
2. In 1907 Nos.104 (March) and 110 (May) were fitted with 5ft 0in. boilers with a firebox 8ft 6in. instead of 7ft 0in. in length. New 19in. cylinders were fitted but still with slide valves, though arranged differently. No.104 kept its new boiler until January 1923. It returned to traffic in June 1923 with the later standard 5ft 0in. superheated boiler, and piston valve cylinders. No.110 passed its boiler to No.113, off May 1918. It then reverted to a 4ft 9in. saturated boiler.
No.113 received 110's boiler in October 1918 and at the same time got new cylinders with piston valves. The boiler was removed in January 1923 (and scrapped, as was No.104's boiler above) and No.113 re-entered service in May 1923 with a 5ft 0in. superheated boiler with 7ft 0in. firebox of the type introduced on the class in 1913 (*see* below).
3. A 5ft 0in. saturated boiler with 7ft 0in. long firebox was built and put on No.1026 in December 1909. New cylinders with piston valves were provided. This boiler was taken off in June 1914, and passed to No.105. No.1026 was ex-works in October 1914 with a 5ft 0in. superheated boiler. No.105 (still with slide valves) was ex-works in August 1914 with No.1026's old boiler. It lasted only until December 1915 when it was removed and scrapped. No.105 then reverted to a 4ft 9in. boiler.
4. In April 1913 No.1021 was given a 5ft 0in. superheated boiler with 7ft 0in. firebox of the type introduced in 1911 on the A5 class 4-6-2T. New cylinders with piston valves, developed from those put in No.1026 in 1909, were fitted.

This was the final development and the entire class were subsequently rebuilt to this form, the last being No.6042 in January 1927.

In most cases new cylinders with piston valves were installed at the same time as the 5ft 0in. superheated boiler, but some engines got new cylinders prior to superheating. They were:

Engine.	New cyls.	Superheated.
1026	12/1909	10/1914
1031	5/1917	4/1922
1027	3/1918	7/1920
112	10/1918	5/1924
113	10/1918	5/1923
1042	11/1922	1/1927

The diameter of the new cylinders was quoted at first as 20in. and the first few had this size. However, 19in. quickly became the standard.

It is almost certain that the boiler numbers for engine numbers 6013 to 6037 at the start of each table are not necessarily those they began with. Sharp Stewart would certainly have applied these in numerical order therefore the

4

One engine built by Kitson in 1887 for the Manchester Exhibition, entered traffic as No.561 in November of that year. By Grouping it had a Robinson chimney and its sandboxes were to GCR standard, but it retained shallow frames, taper shank buffers, and also its different style of footsteps. A No.1 standard boiler with Belpaire firebox was fitted in December 1916. Note that it also had two handles for smokebox door fastening.

This class consisted of three engines all built in 1888. They were numbered 508B, 510B and 511B by Grouping, having changed as shown here to Robinson chimney and GCR No.1 Standard boiler, instead of original with round-top firebox. At re-boilering in 1910/12 the cab roof was extended, and by Grouping parallel shank front buffers had been fitted.

Five engines, Nos.1013 to 1017, were built by Sharp Stewart & Co. in October 1901 for the Great Central Railway. Only No.1014 was named (to honour the Company's Chairman becoming a Baronet in 1902) but from August 1913 it ran without a name, as that had been taken over by the first of the 'Director' class, No.429.

tables probably show the position several years after the engines were built.

At Grouping the entire class carried Robinson's elegant pattern of chimney, those on the 11C and 11D engines naturally being shorter because of their larger boilers. Due to problems caused by cracking, the Robinson chimney was changed to a plain type, followed later by the 'flowerpot' pattern and eventually by a design more akin in shape to the original, but shorter. Lower domes (introduced on the boilers built for the LNER series of Class A5 engines for the North Eastern Area) were adopted as standard on the common Diagram 18 boilers and this meant that Class D9 could be brought within the LNER Composite Load Gauge. All were dealt with by 1939, but whilst the work progressed there were many reversions due to the rotation of boilers still with the taller dome - No.6025 in fact reverted twice during the period 1928-38. The alteration of height to fit either under or over the 13ft. mark was recognised as a class part from 1928. Those over 13ft became Part 1 whilst those under became Part 2. In the tables the various changes are recorded as ' To Part 1' or ' To Part 2'.

From 1919 onwards Ross 'pop' safety valves became standard. The process was gradual and the Ramsbottom type did not disappear until the mid-thirties. Ash ejectors were a standard fitment but were eventually removed, mostly during WW2. Five engines (5112, 6013, 6021, 6040 and 6041) transferred to work on the M&GN lines in 1937 were equipped with tablet exchange apparatus.

Although thirty-four of the original engines were allocated numbers in the 1943 scheme, only twenty-eight of these actually carried numbers in the 2300-2333 range, the others being withdrawn prior to renumbering. Of these, twenty-three went on to acquire the British Railways 6 prefix.

Until the 1928 economies the class were painted by the LNER in the company's green livery. Engines shopped from July of that year received lined out black paintwork. After war broke out, the lining was discontinued from November 1941. Thereafter all remained in plain black except for Nos.62313, 62317 and 62332 which got red, cream and grey lining under BR ownership.

In 1923 three D9's were running with names, which they continued to carry until withdrawal. These were:- No.6021 (later BR No.62307) QUEEN MARY, No.5104 QUEEN ALEXANDRA, and No.5110 KING GEORGE V. In addition, No.6014 had carried the name SIR ALEXANDER but it had been removed in 1913.

Taking their place as the premier passenger motive power on the GC, the D9's worked the fastest trains between Manchester and London over the recently opened 'Extension'. Allocated to Gorton, Leicester and Neasden, the class dominated the workings until the introduction of the Atlantics and D10 'Directors'. From there on, the D9's did much of their work north of Woodford and the majority were concentrated at Sheffield and Annesley by Grouping whilst about ten were divided between Immingham, Lincoln and Retford. Mexborough had also had four D9's but that was prior to 1923 by which time they had gone to either Sheffield or one of the Lincolnshire sheds.

Though relegated in the main to slower passenger turns, they still managed some express work usually between Lincoln and York. Some of the Annesley allocation moved to Colwick, better to serve the Nottingham trains. By the early thirties they were well established in Lincolnshire (as was usual with ex GC 4-4-0's nearing the end of their lives), however, Leicester and Mexborough sheds got a couple during this period, the latter shed having four by 1939. But more suprisingly, the D9's were sent to work in completely alien territory - the G.E. Section -

from 1934 onwards. Ipswich, King's Lynn, March, Norwich and Peterborough East sheds all had one or more D9's on their books during the latter half of the thirties. One of the workings from the latter shed took a D9 into Liverpool Street nearly every other night, a 'Claud' being used alternately.

Another development took place in 1936 when D9's started working over the newly acquired M&GN from Peterborough. South Lynn shed eventually got some D9's allocated as did Yarmouth Beach. At the outbreak of war nearly a third of the class were working in the Eastern Counties, a trend which continued - though numerically less - until 1946 when they left the area and migrated back to their roots.

Prior to WW2 many D9's had started working on the Cheshire Lines, being stationed at Brunswick and Trafford Park sheds and from which places they held reign over the fast trains between Liverpool and Manchester. Heaton Mersey also had a couple and by the end of the LNER the twenty-seven surviving D9's were all working on the CLC. Nearing old age at the start of BR, the engines were gradually whittled down so that by mid 1950 the last example, No.62305 was withdrawn spelling the demise of the D9's.

D10

Just ten engines made up the GCR Class 11E 4-4-0 design (LNER Class D10) but they were to prove to be superb locomotives for their intended work and were a gigantic improvement on the same designers D9's. The D10's were built at Gorton, being turned out during the latter months of 1913. A further order was placed for another batch of 'Directors' in 1916 but wartime constraints led to cancellation, however, in 1919 the order was again issued but with detail alterations to the original design. This order led to the introduction of the 'Improved Directors' (GC Class 11F) of which more later.

The basic design of boiler was shared with classes D11 and L1 (L3), though initially there were detail differences. It was known as No.5 Standard at Gorton and became LNER Diagram 14. The number of superheater elements was twenty-four but on D10, when built, they were of the short loop type and the number of small tubes was 175. Long loop elements, together with 157 tubes, were introduced on Class L1 when new (in 1914) and this type became standard. L1 alone had the top feed, taken off by the LNER not long after Grouping (see also Volume 21). Thereafter the boiler design became standard on all three classes.

Numbered 429 to 438 in the GC fleet, all ten acquired names and these were appropriately after the Company's own Directors. No.429 was at first named SIR ALEXANDER HENDERSON. However, he was elevated to the peerage as Lord Faringdon and his new title was bestowed on the first of the Great Central's 4-cylinder 4-6-0's (LNER B3), whereupon in 1917 No.429 became SIR DOUGLAS HAIG (the military C-in-C). He in turn received an earldom in 1919 and his name was promoted to another B3. No.429 itself then received promotion, this time to royalty, as PRINCE HENRY (the Duke of Gloucester). Likewise No.437 became PRINCE GEORGE (the Duke of Kent) in 1920 after CHARLES STUART WORTLEY (its previous name) was created a baron and duly moved to yet another B3.

Although the running plate was raised over the coupled wheels, the lower edge of the valance was not, thus reducing accessibility to the coupling rod journals. During 1925-26 this unnecessary plating (a feature also of Class D11) was removed.

No attempt was made to bring Class D10 within the LNER Composite Load Gauge, chimney, dome and cab all being higher than permitted. However, by 1930 the Robinson chimney had been changed on the whole class to the Gresley 'flowerpot' type, only to be soon replaced by a shortened version of the original pattern. Domes too were reduced in height on replacement boilers, a standard imposed in connection with the D11/2 engines. The cab height was never altered. It may be mentioned that in practice the only sections of the LNER system that were barred to the 'Directors' were the GE and Scottish, the GN and NE and of course their native lines presenting no problem in respect of load gauge.

The LNER quickly painted Class D10 in lined out green livery and eight of the class received the early C suffix to their numbers. From November 1928 they fell victim to the economy campaign and thereafter were turned out in black, with single red lining until 1941.

Under BR ownership No.62658 was repainted in fully lined out black in August 1948 in connection with its appearance at an exhibition. Subsequently in 1952 Nos.62652, 62653 and 62656 also received this livery, but the rest remained without lining through to withdrawal.

Sent initially to work the expresses on the Extension from Neasden, the class quickly built up a reputation for speed and free steaming before wartime stringencys put a damper on their capabilities. However, they excelled in the work thrown at them during the period of hostilities. At the end of the war No.434 moved to Gorton for a while but went back to London to join the others. Shortly after this the 'Improved Directors' started to arrive from Gorton and all eleven of that class ended up at Neasden to the detriment of the 'Directors' of which more than half of that class were sent away, initially to Sheffield and Woodford, but by Grouping to Gorton with only three resident at Neasden. They were though still working many of the expresses between Manchester and London. Once all the 'Improved Directors' had been put into traffic and taken up residence at Neasden, the remaining 'Directors' moved to Gorton then Annesley from which shed they worked a morning Mansfield to London express as far as Leicester. In 1924 Annesley lost its 'Directors' to Gorton from where they could still do much useful work and from there they went to Neasden again working alongside the D11's of which a number had gone to Gorton, swapped for D10's.

No.5435 was the first D10 to be allocated to Brunswick shed, in 1927, but only for just over a year; its main job there was working to Sheffield with a Hull train via Stockport. The same engine went to Neepsend shed in 1931 and where in 1933 it was joined by No.5431 which had had a six month stint at Copley Hill shed. Two more D10's went to Leeds in 1933 and they remained there until 1938. In 1936 both Gorton and Neasden gave up the bulk of their allocation of D10's to Sheffield Neepsend, the one exception, No.5437, stayed in London for another year before moving to Annesley where its main job was main line pilot at Nottingham (Victoria) which it shared with No.5431. By mid 1939 all the class were at Neepsend, a situation which lasted until the following February when two of the class went to Mexborough until August 1943. During this same period Sheffield gave up three D10's to Doncaster but these returned to Sheffield (by now the new shed at Darnall) at the same time as Mexborough sent its pair back.

Until 1946 Darnall kept hold of all the D10's but in May of that year No.5435 went once again to Brunswick but only for a few months this time. However, the next year saw seven of the class move to the Cheshire Lines and these were joined two years later by the remaining three from Darnall. They put in good work from Brunswick, Trafford Park and Northwich sheds, but once on the CLC their days were numbered and between March 1953 and October 1955 all ten were withdrawn.

D11/1

In a bid to improve still further his Class 11E 4-4-0 design, J.G.Robinson brought out the GCR Class 11F in 1919. Numbered 506, the pioneer engine was the first of eleven locomotives which eventually made up the class known as the 'Improved Directors' - LNER Class D11. The first five, Nos.506 to 510, were turned out from Gorton in the period between December 1919 and May 1920. These were followed in the latter quarter of 1922 by six more numbered 501 to 505 and 511.

The 11F was essentially a 'Director' but with, as the pseudonym implied, improvements to the original design. The most significant was a new layout for the cylinders incorporating the more conventional inside admission of steam to the piston valves, rather than outside as used on the D9 and D10 engines. The main frames at the front end were redesigned and the boiler was pitched $1\frac{1}{2}$ ins. higher with attendant reduction in the height of the chimney. The most noticeable external change was to the cab which now had side windows and a rearward extension to the roof. Until 1937 no major improvements were made to the D11's but in January of that year Gresley had No.5505 fitted with new cylinders equipped with long travel valves. Eventually all but the pioneer engine got this modification, most during the 1940's but the last one was not carried out until February 1952 when No.62665 emerged from Gorton. Most of the D11/2's were also subject to the cylinder change (see below).

Detail changes largely kept in step with those made to Class D10, the deep valances over the coupled wheels being removed in 1925-26 and the ash ejectors during WW2.

Changes to chimneys and dome also followed those outlined above under Class D10 although No.5507 carried a short cast chimney from March 1924 believed to be experimental in connection with the introduction of Class D11/2. Like Class D10, the dimensions of the cab remained outside the LNER load gauge so that the same restrictions on their sphere of operation applied.

The first two engines, Nos.506 and 507, bore the names of the only two GCR Directors not already so honoured, whilst the next three were named after the eldest children of King George V and Queen Mary. During LNER days No.5508 PRINCE OF WALES duplicated Gresley Pacific No.2553 (renamed thus in December 1926) and this anomaly was never rectified. The names on the 1922 batch of D11's all commemorated WW1 battles, four of them duplicating those carried by NBR J36 0-6-0 engines.

Although Nos.503, 504, 505 and 511 were put to stock by the GCR late in 1922, they did not receive their final painting until early in 1923. Thus they got GCR livery but carried LNER lettering. The whole class were later painted LNER green but fell victim to the economies introduced in June 1928 whereby, when next shopped, they came out in black with single red lining, the latter dropped from November 1941. Under BR they remained in black but starting with No.62669 in May 1952, this was lined out. The whole class is believed to have been so treated during the next three years. Those shopped from October 1956 lost the lining, these being Nos.62660, 62663, 62666, 62667 and 62670.

As pointed out above, the D11's basically ousted the D10's from Neasden and took over much of the main line work but from 1924 six of the class went to Gorton in exchange for D10's. At Gorton the D11's took on much the same duties on the main line to Leicester but also had workings to Sheffield and Retford. In February 1927 Gorton sent No.5511 to Copley Hill for Pullman train working from Harrogate to King's Cross. These runs were of an experimental nature at first but the D11 soon proved its potential with the lightly loaded trains and became a regular and popular performer, sharing the opposite working with C1's. In April, No.5507 joined No.5511 at Copley Hill to work the same duties and various D11's continued doing so for another five years, No.5507 staying at the Leeds shed throughout the period. In May 1932 the D11's reign on the Pullman workings came to an end because the timing became tighter with less for recovery which the 4-4-0's found difficulty with compared to the 4-4-2's and the D11 coal consumption was somewhat more than the Atlantics with which they shared the work.

Neasden shed received the three given up by Copley Hill and the D11's joined in the workings on the Manchester expresses with their Gorton counterparts. In 1936 the influx of new B17's onto the former GC main line saw the D11's being left out of the top link work and they became somewhat surplus. Some were sent to Sheffield and others were put into store. No.5508 ended up at Immingham in January 1940, previous transfers having taken it to Retford and then Lincoln; the engine spent all of the war years stationed at Immingham. Langwith and Mexborough sheds gained some of the D11's during the war years. In the latter years of the LNER three sheds shared the class with Mexborough and Neasden having four each and Immingham the balance. On the eve of nationalisation the latter shed housed all eleven of the D11/1's.

As was customary with elderly GC 4-4-0 engines and despite the fact that the section was by now under control of the London Midland Region, the whole class had moved in 1950 to various sheds on the Cheshire Lines but within no time eight of them were in store at Trafford Park. In 1952 Northwich shed got one of the stored engines and in the following year two left for Immingham and then on to Mexborough. Later on the storage lines saw all but one of the D11's depart for greener pastures, at least for the time being. During 1953-57 several were allocated to the former Midland Railway shed at Lincoln (by then under Eastern Region control) whence they worked via Newark to Nottingham. However, the D11's found regular employment difficult and from 1957 storage became an all to familiar option for them with both Darnall and Staveley sheds storing them. Withdrawal had started with No.62665 in May 1959 but other members of the class found occasional summer work in between stints on the storage tracks. Like so many other steam locomotives of the period, 1960 proved to be the final year for the remaining D11's and in December the last one No.62666 was condemned.

When No.62660 (formerly No.506) BUTLER-HENDERSON was withdrawn in November 1960 it was preserved as part of the National Collection. Now, beautifully restored, it can be seen at Loughborough where it operates on its former territory.

D12

This former GCR double-framed 4-4-0 class had been introduced in 1877 by the then Manchester, Sheffield & Lincolnshire Railway's Locomotive Engineer Charles Sacré. It was the first 4-4-0 type used by the MSLR and twelve, Nos.423 to 434, were built at Gorton in 1877. In the following year another ten, Nos.435 to 444, were turned out from Gorton with two more, Nos.445 and 446 in 1879 and finally three in 1880; these last three, Nos.4, 128 and 129, 'bucked the trend' of the successive numbering which up to then had been the case.

Of the original twenty-seven GCR Class 6B, twelve had survived to Grouping and most of these were forty-five or more years old so their future on the LNER did not look too good from the start. However, there was no mass condemnation of the class and the engines simply went for scrap in one's and two's, the last one as late as 1930.

During their lifetime the engines had received new boilers, still with round top firebox, and a few detail changes but otherwise they were largely as built, reflecting the 1870's trend of British express locomotive design. They had received three different chimneys, the original Sacré type, his successor Parker's stovepipe design and finally the standard Robinson chimney, all surmounting the different smokeboxes carried by the class.

Withdrawals of the D12's had started in GC days though the class had stayed intact up to 1919, all being put onto the GC Duplicate List by 1914; they had been relegated to menial and secondary duties long before 1900.

When introduced the engines worked the Manchester to London expresses as far as Retford where the Great Northern took over responsibility for the trains. Both Gorton and Retford sheds shared these duties with the larger allocation at the former shed which also provided D12's for the Manchester-Sheffield services. Neepsend shed also had a handful of these engines. However, the longest workings carried out by the class was on the Liverpool-Hull services and for this Brunswick shed had seven D12's with another permanently outstationed at Hull. By the mid eighties the Sacré single-wheelers became the preferred motive power on the London trains which now took the MS&LR engine down to Grantham before handover to GN power. The D12's continued putting in good work on the Hull and Sheffield services at this period and besides those, they performed well on the Cheshire Lines fastest trains between Liverpool and Manchester.

In their twilight years on the GCR, five of the class were loaned to the Great North of Scotland Railway for a period of just over six months from June 1920 but most of their work there involved the goods traffic as none were Westinghouse fitted.

Shortly before Grouping the survivors were scattered over most of the northern area of the GC system and one, No.442B, was even stationed as far south as Leicester but only doing light work.

Of the twelve to reach Grouping, seven were allocated numbers in the 1924 renumbering taking up numbers in the 646X series but only four are thought to have been so numbered, the others being scrapped with their GC Duplicate List numbers.

The last members of the class worked from New Holland and Annesley sheds, the latter establishment providing work for the final survivor No.6464 (442B) which shared the Annesley Dido workings with other ancient and non-standard engines sent to the Nottinghamshire shed for such duties. No.6464 was withdrawn in March 1930 the penultimate Sacré engine working on the LNER.

Ten engines Nos.429 to 438, were built at Gorton between August and December 1913. All were named after GCR Directors. As built, the superheater element protection was by Robinson draught retarder and there was a Wakefield mechanical lubricator for the cylinders and piston valves. Four-column Ramsbottom safety valves were fitted and there was a carriage heater connection at the front. Manchester (London Road).

Five engines, Nos.506, 507, 508, 509 and 510, built at Gorton between December 1919 and May 1920 became LNER Class D11. The running plate had a full valance to the raised portion and Ross 'pop' safety valves were fitted as standard from building. The cab roof had a rear extension to provide better protection for the crew.

This class originally comprised twenty-seven engines built at Gorton during the period 1877 to 1880. Apart from a change of chimney from stovepipe to Robinson design, and the removal of the smokebox wing-plates, they underwent very little change.

By Grouping, all six D5's had been fitted with longer smokebox but were not superheated. Note only two washout plugs on this side. For work on the London Extension, a 4000 gallon tender with coping has been fitted, but at Grouping only Nos.698 and 699 retained the large tender, the other four having reverted to 3080 gallon type.

(left) The original boilers were all replaced between 1906 and 1916 by the GCR Standard No.3 boiler, and the later ones had the Ramsbottom safety valves mounted directly on to the firebox, enclosed by a cast iron cover. No.694 got this boiler in July 1913 but reverted to small tender in January 1922. Note change on the firebox to two plugs and two handholes.

(below) After Grouping it was decided that 4000 gallon tenders were more useful on this class and so the four with the smaller type again got the 4000 gallon type taken from J10 class goods engines. These were fitted to Nos.5694 (11/25), 5695 (6/26), 5696 (11/27) and 5697 (12/24). When coupled to D5 class they were still without any coal guard.

CLASS D 5

5694

Gorton.

To traffic 7/1895.

REPAIRS:
Gor. ?/?—?/7/13.**G.**
Gor. 26/2—26/3/21.**G.**
Gor. 23/6—27/10/23.**G.**
Gor. 4/7—14/11/25.**G.**
Superheated boiler fitted.
Gor. 5/11/27—7/1/28.**G.**
Gor. 8/3—12/4/30.**G.**
Gor. 31/10/32. *Not repaired.*

BOILERS:
88 ?/7/13
172 *(sup.)* 14/11/25.

SHEDS:
Trafford Park.
Walton-on-the-Hill.
Trafford Park 17/2/28.

RENUMBERED:
694c 17/11/23.
5694 14/11/25.

CONDEMNED: 31/10/32.
Cut up at Gorton.

5695

Gorton.

To traffic 8/1895.

REPAIRS:
Gor. ?/?—?/?/13.**G.**
Gor. 8/6—17/8/18.**G.**
Gor. 28/8—13/11/20.**G.**
Gor. 14/7—29/9/23.**G.**
Gor. 1/5—14/8/26.**G.**
Superheated boiler fitted.
Gor. 16/3—20/4/29.**G.**
Gor. 18/7/31. *Not repaired.*

BOILERS:
1119 *(exD6 881)* ?/13.
135 17/8/18.
693 *(sup.)* 14/8/26.

SHEDS:
Trafford Park.
Walton-on-the-Hill.
Trafford Park 17/2/28.

RENUMBERED:
695c 20/10/23.
5695 14/8/26.

CONDEMNED: 18/7/31.
Cut up at Gorton.

5696

Gorton.

To traffic 10/1895.

REPAIRS:
Gor. ?/?—?/3/16.**G.**
Gor. 26/2—16/7/21.**G.**
Gor. 22/3—21/6/24.**G.**
Gor. 1/10—12/11/27.**G.**
Gor. 25/7/30. *Not repaired.*

BOILERS:
1227 ?/3/16.
622 16/7/21.
1122 12/11/27.

SHEDS:
Trafford Park.
Walton-on-the-Hill.
Trafford Park 17/2/28.

RENUMBERED:
5696 21/6/24.

CONDEMNED: 25/7/30.
Cut up at Gorton.

5697

Gorton.

To traffic 10/1895.

REPAIRS:
Gor. ?/?—?/9/06.**G.**
Gor. 13/8/21—28/1/22.**G.**
Gor. 30/8—6/12/24.**G.**
Gor. 10/12/27—28/1/28.**G.**
Gor. 19/7—30/8/30.**G.**
Gor. 21/10/32. *Not repaired.*

BOILERS:
1229 *(new)* ?/9/06.

SHEDS:
Trafford Park.
Walton-on-the-Hill.
Trafford Park 17/2/28.

RENUMBERED:
5697 6/12/24.

CONDEMNED: 21/10/32.
Cut up at Gorton.

5698

Gorton.

To traffic 11/1895.

REPAIRS:
Gor. ?/?—?/?/13 .**G.**
Gor. 22/11/19—13/11/20.**G.**
Gor. 14/7—1/9/23.**G.**
Gor. 2/10—11/12/26.**G.**
Gor. 16/2—16/3/29.**G.**
Gor. 3/10/31. *Not repaired.*

BOILERS:
1122 ?/?/13.
135 11/12/26.

SHEDS:
Trafford Park.
Walton-on-the-Hill.
Trafford Park 17/2/28.

RENUMBERED:
698c 22/9/23.
5698 *by* 9/2/26.

CONDEMNED: 3/10/31.
Cut up at Doncaster.

5699

Gorton.

To traffic 12/1895.

REPAIRS:
Gor. 25/11/08—16/1/09.**G.**
Gor. 2/10/15—29/1/16.**G.**
Gor. 4/9—9/10/20.**G.**
Gor. 10/3—14/4/23.**G.**
Gor. 26/9—28/11/25.**G.**
Gor. 25/2—31/3/28.**G.**
Gor. 6/12/30—10/1/31.**G.**
Gor. 25/3/33. *Not repaired.*

BOILERS:
130 16/1/09.
176 29/1/16.
88 28/11/25.

SHEDS:
Trafford Park.
Walton-on-the-Hill.
Trafford Park 3/3/28.

RENUMBERED:
5699 28/11/25.

CONDEMNED: 25/3/33.
Cut up at Gorton.

Only two were superheated: Nos.5694 (14/11/25) and 5695 (14/8/26). The chimney was moved forward to clear the header and sight feed lubrication from the cab was provided. On 5695 there was no external evidence of any protection for the superheater elements, but 5694 had an anti-vacuum valve at both ends of the header. At its April 1929 repair, No.5695's tender got square ended coal guards but without any beading. Gorton.

The Robinson chimney was only removed from two: Nos.5694 and 5699 getting the 'plantpot' type in November 1925. Note 5699 lost its cover around the safety valves.

By the end of 1924 all six were in LNER green passenger livery, No.699 was out 2nd June 1923 as L.&N.E.R. The next three got the C suffix 698 (22/9/23), 695 (20/10/23), 694 (17/11/23). The other two 5696 (21/6/24) and 5697 (6/12/24) went straight to 1924 numbering. No.5696 kept its green painting to withdrawal on 25th July 1930. Manchester (Central).

In the June 1928 economies D5 was to lose the green and to get black with single red lining. This was applied to 5698 (16/3/29) and to 5695 (20/4/29) in both cases the number remaining on the tender, and still there when withdrawn in 1931.

When the other three became black, the number was moved to the cab and 12in. LNER was then used on the tender. These three were 5694 (12/4/30), 5697 (30/8/30) and 5699 (10/1/31).

Two engines, Nos.268 (September) and 269 (December), were built at Gorton in 1897. Between April and December 1898 they were followed by eleven more, Nos.852 to 861 and No.270. No.269 is shown here with its post-1912 extension to the cab roof and boiler built in 1905 and used June 1918 to March 1927, after which this engine was superheated.

The remaining twenty engines of D6 class, Nos.862 to 881, were built from December 1898 to April 1899 by Beyer, Peacock (see page 2). No.876 shown here with superheated boiler put on in March 1913 had a steam circulating valve on the smokebox and a Wakefield mechanical lubricator was provided for cylinders and valves. Note the two washout plugs, also the two handholes on the shoulder of the firebox. The later GC design buffers with parallel shanks are fitted. This was one of the four D6 (Nos.857, 859 and 869 were the others) to have Westinghouse brake added in 1902/3 for train working.

CLASS D 6

5268

Gorton.

To traffic 9/1897.

REPAIRS:
Gor. ?/?—12/4/06.**G.**
Gor. 12/12/14—30/1/15.**G.**
Superheated boiler fitted.
Gor. 3/6—8/7/22.**L.**
Gor. 15/11/24—31/1/25.**G.**
Gor. 5/3—7/5/27.**G.**
Gor. 24/11/28—12/1/29.**G.**
Gor. 18/4—16/5/31.**G.**
Gor. 19/7/33. *Not repaired.*

BOILERS:
242 12/4/06.
900 *(sup.)* 30/1/15.
 62 7/5/27.

SHEDS:
Brunswick.
Heaton Mersey 23/9/29.
Brunswick 6/2/33.

RENUMBERED:
5268 31/1/25.

CONDEMNED: 19/7/33.
Cut up at Gorton.

5269

Gorton.

To traffic 12/1897.

REPAIRS:
Gor. 11/4—8/6/08.**G.**
Gor. 27/4—15/6/18.**G.**
Gor. 24/7—4/9/20.**G.**
Gor. 3/2—7/4/23.**G.**
Gor. 28/6—9/8/24.**G.**
Gor. 5/3—7/5/27.**G.**
Superheated boiler fitted.
Gor. 12/1—16/2/29.**G.**
Gor. 7/2—7/3/31.**G.**
Gor. 2/11/32. *Not repaired.*

BOILERS:
 430 8/6/08.
1137 15/6/18.
1824 *(sup.)* 7/5/27.

SHEDS:
Walton-on-the-Hill.
Brunswick 18/2/28.
Heaton Mersey 23/9/29.

RENUMBERED:
5269 9/8/24.

CONDEMNED: 2/11/32.
Cut up at Gorton.

5852

Gorton.

To traffic 4/1898.

REPAIRS:
Gor. 14/3—30/5/08.**G.**
Gor. 1/12/17—16/2/18.**G.**
Gor. 21/5—15/10/21.**G.**
Superheated boiler fitted.
Gor. 26/4—19/7/24.**G.**
Gor. 18/9—18/12/26.**G.**
Gor. 19—26/3/27.**L.**
Chimney alterations.
Gor. 22/9—27/10/28.**G.**
Gor. 15/11—20/12/30.**G.**
Gor. 13—27/8/32.**G.**
Gor. 23/2—9/3/35.**G.**
Gor. 14/11—5/12/36.**G.**

BOILERS:
238 30/5/08.
242 16/2/18.
904 *(sup.)* 15/10/21.
247 27/10/28.
110 27/8/32.
746 9/3/35.
973 5/12/36.

SHEDS:
Trafford Park *at* 14/8/23.
Brunswick *by* 12/28.
Trafford Park 7/11/32.
Brunswick 7/4/33.
Gorton 27/12/36.
Trafford Park 3/7/37.

RENUMBERED:
5852 19/7/24.

CONDEMNED: 2/6/38.
Into Gor. for cut up 4/6/38.

5853

Gorton.

To traffic 5/1898.

REPAIRS:
Gor. ?/?—1/7/05.**G.**
Gor. 13/12/13—4/4/14.**G.**
Superheated boiler fitted.
Gor. 8/4—12/8/22.**G.**
Gor. 1/11/24—21/3/25.**G.**
Gor. 23/10/26—8/1/27.**G.**
Gor. 7/7—4/8/28.**G.**
Gor. 19/4—24/5/30.**G.**
Gor. 6—27/2/32.**G.**
Gor. 3—24/2/34.**G.**
Gor. 1—22/2/36.**G.**
Gor. 1—22/1/38.**G.**
Gor. 10—31/8/40.**G.**
Gor. 12—23/10/43.**G.**
Gor. 16/3/46. *Not repaired.*

BOILERS:
282 1/7/05.
 89 *(sup.)* 4/4/14.
1589 4/8/28.
519 27/2/32.
688 24/2/34.
732 22/2/36.
697 22/1/38.
975 31/8/40.
739 23/10/43.

SHEDS:
Trafford Park 11/2/21.
Brunswick 7/7/33.
Trafford Park 9/6/38.
Heaton Mersey 22/10/38.
Gorton 7/12/39.
Brunswick 17/1/40.

RENUMBERED:
5853 21/3/25.
***2100** allocated.*

CONDEMNED: 4/4/46.
Cut up at Gorton.

5854

Gorton.

To traffic 6/1898.

REPAIRS:
Gor. ?/?—4/5/12.**G.**
Superheated boiler fitted.
Gor. 12/10/18—11/1/19.**G.**
Gor. 16/12/22—10/2/23.**G.**
Gor. 7/6—9/8/24.**G.**
Gor. 11/7—10/10/25.**G.**
Gor. 16/7—3/9/27.**G.**
Gor. 16/3—20/4/29.**G.**
Gor. 2/5/31. *Not repaired.*

BOILERS:
 247 *(new, sup.)* 4/5/12.
1723 11/1/19.
909 20/4/29.

SHED:
Trafford Park.

RENUMBERED:
5854 9/8/24.

CONDEMNED: 2/5/31.
Cut up at Gorton.

5855

Gorton.

To traffic 7/1898.

REPAIRS:
Gor. ?/?—27/8/04.**G.**
Gor. 24/8—9/10/09.**G.**
Gor. 14/7—30/12/11.**G.**
Gor. 21/2—20/6/14.**G.**
Superheated boiler fitted.
Gor. 15/7—7/10/22.**G.**
Gor. 1/11/24—7/2/25.**G.**
Gor. 23/10/26—8/1/27.**G.**
Gor. 8/10—10/12/27.**G.**
Gor. 29/3—17/5/30.**G.**
New frames & cylinders.
Gor. 21/5—4/6/32.**G.**
Gor. 3—31/3/34.**G.**
Gor. 4—18/1/36.**G.**
Gor. 4—25/12/37.**G.**
Gor. 4—11/2/39.**L.**
Gor. 2—23/9/39.**G.**
Gor. 16/6—4/7/42.**G.**
Gor. 28/10/44.**L.**
Gor. 6—20/10/45.**G.**

BOILERS:
1058.
1058 27/8/04.
 904 9/10/09.
1058 30/12/11.
 206 *(sup.)* 20/6/14.
 757 7/2/25.
 110 17/5/30.
 436 4/6/32.
 660 31/3/34.
 697 18/1/36.
4512 25/12/37.
 971 23/9/39.
 743 4/7/42.
 365 20/10/45.

SHEDS:
Trafford Park 27/9/04.
Heaton Mersey 29/3/34.
Trafford Park 13/7/35.
Heaton Mersey 10/1/38.

No.878 with boiler built in 1909 which this engine carried from December 1909 to February 1929, remaining non-superheated. This was one of the few GCR No.3 standard boilers which did not have a superheater. In 1909-11, four engines, Nos.857, 863, 866 and 878 were fitted with a slightly longer smokebox. Manchester (London Rd.)

When taken over by the LNER only five of the 33 engines, Nos.269, 866, 867, 878 and 880 were not superheated and No.5878 was not so equipped until March 1934, although having a boiler change in February 1929, when it got Ramsbottom safety valves mounted directly on the firebox casing. Gorton shed.

In August 1913, when a superheater was put in, No.858 was also fitted with a Galloway-Hill furnace in the firebox in which steam jets were used. The steam supply pipe was taken from the left hand side of the smokebox. When No.858 went into works 2nd September 1922, this device was removed. Trafford Park.

Although No.866 did not get a superheater until April 1927, it had clearly been prepared to be so fitted before Grouping as both a frame extension and full length smokebox were provided. Instead, it continued to carry a 1911 built No.3 standard saturated boiler. Note displacement type lubricator fitted for piston valves. Trafford Park.

Before the LNER took over, protection of superheater elements from burning did not rate highly. The twenty superheated to January 1915, apart from the first one No.854, were originally provided with draught retarders as shown on No.876 on page 14, but these had been removed by 1923, only the bracket on the smokebox remaining. Seven more, superheated in 1916-21, had no element protection provided. Gorton shed.

5855 cont./
Gorton 28/7/39.
Heaton Mersey 24/9/39.
Chester 7/5/42.
Walton-on-the-Hill 3/1/43.
Brunswick 7/11/43.
Northwich 11/8/46.

RENUMBERED:
5855 7/2/25.
2101 5/5/46.

CONDEMNED: 16/12/47.
Into Gor. for cut up 20/12/47
but cut up at Dukinfield.

5856

Gorton.

To traffic 8/1898.

REPAIRS:
Gor. 14/10—28/11/08.**G.**
Gor. 25/3—25/11/11.**G.**
Gor. 19/6—31/7/15.**G.**
Gor. 14/5—18/6/21.**G.**
Superheated boiler fitted.
Gor. 22/3—31/5/24.**G.**
Gor. 25/9/26—8/1/27.**G.**
Gor. 1/9—20/10/28.**G.**
Gor. 6/12/30—3/1/31.**G.**
Gor. 30/4—21/5/32.**G.**
Gor. 16/12/33—13/1/34.**G.**
Gor. 20/7—17/8/35.**G.**
Gor. 20/3—10/4/37.**G.**
Gor. 12/1/39. *Not repaired.*

BOILERS:
791 28/11/08.
400 25/11/11.
622 31/7/15.
1081 *(sup.)* 18/6/21.
1840 3/1/31.
674 21/5/32.
361 13/1/34.
741 17/8/35.
971 10/4/37.

SHEDS:
Trafford Park.
Immingham 10/2/38.

RENUMBERED:
5856 31/5/24.

CONDEMNED: 12/1/39.
Cut up at Gorton.

5857

Gorton.

To traffic 8/1898.

REPAIRS:
Gor. 28/8/15—1/1/16.**G.**
Superheated boiler fitted.
Gor. 21/10—30/12/22.**G.**
Gor. 21/2—30/5/25.**G.**
Gor. 4/6—30/7/27.**G.**
Gor. 3—17/3/28.**G.**
Gor. 31/8—12/10/29.**G.**
Gor. 25/7/31. *Not repaired.*

BOILERS:
1589 *(sup.)* 1/1/16.
297 30/7/27.

SHED:
Trafford Park.

RENUMBERED:
5857 30/5/25.

CONDEMNED: 8/8/31.
Cut up at Gorton.

5858

Gorton.

To traffic 9/1898.

REPAIRS:
Gor. ?/?—2/8/13.**G.**
Superheated boiler fitted.
Gor. 2/9/22—13/1/23.**G.**
Gor. 6/12/24—21/2/25.**G.**
Gor. 13/2—17/4/26.**G.**
Gor. 26/11/27—28/1/28.**G.**
Gor. 5/10—2/11/29.**G.**
Gor. 14/11/31. *Not repaired.*

BOILERS:
95 *(new. sup.)* 2/8/13.
976 2/11/29.

SHED:
Trafford Park.

RENUMBERED:
5858 21/2/25.

CONDEMNED: 14/11/31.
Cut up at Gorton.

5859

Gorton.

To traffic 10/1898.

REPAIRS:
Gor. 15/9—7/11/08.**G.**
Gor. 25/11/10—17/2/11.**G.**
Gor. 29/4—7/10/16.**G.**
Superheated boiler fitted.
Gor. 28/1—15/4/22.**G.**
Gor. 19/7—22/11/24.**G.**
Gor. 1/5—31/7/26.**G.**
Gor. 10/5—9/8/30.**G.**
New frames & cylinders.
Gor. 30/4—14/5/32.**G.**
Westinghouse brake removed.
Gor. 21—28/10/33.**G.**
Gor. 22/6—6/7/35.**G.**
Gor. 8—29/5/37.**G.**
Gor. 3—24/12/38.**G.**
Gor. 16—30/11/40.**G.**
Gor. 12—30/10/43.**G.**
Gor. 16/12/44—13/1/45.**L.**

BOILERS:
567 7/11/08.
586 17/2/11.
1623 *(sup.)* 7/10/16.
755 22/11/24.
189 14/5/32.
971 28/10/33.
161 6/7/35.
693 29/5/37.
4510 24/12/38.
697 30/11/40.
731 30/10/43.

SHEDS:
Brunswick 22/7/21.
Trafford Park 10/2/38.
Heaton Mersey 20/8/38.
Brunswick 25/12/38.
Gorton 10/6/39.
Heaton Mersey 28/7/39.
Northwich 7/6/42.

RENUMBERED:
5859 22/11/24.
2102 *allocated.*

CONDEMNED: 28/9/45.
Into Gor. for cut up 29/9/45.

5860

Gorton.

To traffic 11/1898.

REPAIRS:
Gor. ?/?—19/7/13.**G.**
Superheated boiler fitted.
Gor. 21/2—1/5/20.**G**
Gor. 28/1—25/3/22.**G.**
Gor. 10/2—12/5/23.**G.**
Gor. 5/9—19/12/25.**G.**
Gor. 17/3—12/5/28.**G.**
Gor. 16/11/29—4/1/30.**G.**
Gor. 14/11/31. *Not repaired.*

BOILERS:
172 *(new. sup.)* 19/7/13.
110 1/5/20.
436 19/12/25.

SHED:
Trafford Park.

RENUMBERED:
5860 19/12/25.

CONDEMNED: 14/11/31.
Cut up at Gorton.

5861

Gorton.

To traffic 11/1898.

REPAIRS:
Gor. 4/9/15—19/2/16.**G.**
Superheated boiler fitted.
Gor. 26/6—7/8/20.**G.**
Gor. 3—24/2/23.**G.**
Gor. 14/2—25/4/25.**G.**
Gor. 30/7—24/12/27.**G.**
Gor. 29/12/28—2/2/29.**G.**
Gor. 20/4/31. *Not repaired.*

BOILERS:
1595 *(sup.)* 19/2/16.
89 2/2/29.

SHED:
Trafford Park.

RENUMBERED:
5861 25/4/25.

CONDEMNED: 20/4/31.
Cut up at Gorton.

5270

Gorton.

To traffic 12/1898.

WORKS CODES:- Bpk - Beyer, Peacock. Cow - Cowlairs. Dar- Darlington. Don - Doncaster. Efd - Eastfield. Ghd - Gateshead. Gor - Gorton. Inv - Inverurie. Str - Stratford. Wfd - Woodford.
REPAIR CODES:- **C/H** - Casual Heavy. **C/L** - Casual Light. **G** - General. **H**- Heavy. **H/I** - Heavy Intermediate. **L** - Light. **L/I** - Light Intermediate. **N/C** - Non-Classified.

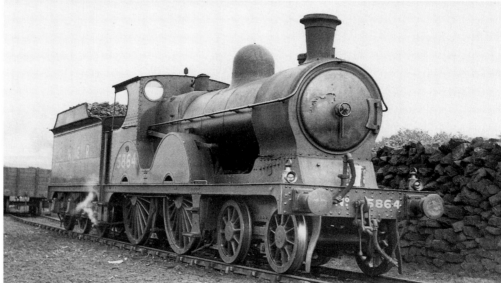

(above) **No.854 was the first to be superheated and official photographs show it was provided with superheater dampers with control through the handrail alongside the boiler. Draught retarders were substituted although these too had been removed by 1923. All superheated engines got the Wakefield mechanical lubricator for pistons and valves.**

(centre) **Beginning with No.5864 in April 1925 and No.5880 in January 1926, Gresley anti-vacuum valves were introduced, and two were fitted, one at each end of the header, an arrangement which was still in use up to 1940. By 1930, however, the normal central position for a single valve had been standardised.**

No.5869 with the two anti-vacuum valves as first supplied. Note the Wakefield mechanical lubricator mounted on the frame ahead of the front splasher on the left side. All except No.859 (in October 1916) were fitted with the Wakefield type; No.859 got the Intensifore sight feed lubricator when superheated but this was removed in favour of a Wakefield type in July 1935.

Where two valves had been carried, the smokebox was patched when the change to central anti-vacuum valve was made.

Until November 1924 all the class were well over the 13ft 0in. composite load gauge with both the Robinson chimney and dome stud. In November 1924, No.5859 got a new boiler with 'plantpot' chimney and a shorter dome cover both of which were within the composite gauge. All 33 duly changed to the 'plantpot' chimney but ten, Nos.5268, 5269, 5854, 5857, 5860, 5861, 5862, 5866, 5868 and 5872, were withdrawn between September 1930 (5866) and July 1933 (5268) still with the original full height dome. Brunswick shed.

(below) The other 23 were all duly brought within the 13ft 0in. load gauge, No.5856 in August 1935 being the last to be altered.

5270 cont./
REPAIRS:
Gor. ?/?—21/4/06.**G.**
Gor. 2—30/1/15.**G.**
Superheated boiler fitted.
Gor. 28/1—25/2/22.**G.**
Gor. 20/1—24/2/23.**G.**
Gor. 7/2—16/5/25.**G.**
Gor. 24/9/27—3/3/28.**G.**
Gor. 8/2—8/3/30.**G.**
Gor. 31/12/31—16/1/32.**G.**
Gor. 18/11—2/12/33.**G.**
Gor. 12—26/10/35.**G.**
Gor. 19/6—3/7/37.**G.**
Gor. 11/5—1/6/40.**G.**
Gor. 30/1—27/2/43.**G.**
Gor. 20—25/12/43.**L.**
Tender only.
Gor. 21/4/45. *Not repaired.*

BOILERS:
622 21/4/06.
909 *(sup.)* 30/1/15.
110 3/3/28.
757 8/3/30.
742 16/1/32.
697 2/12/33.
1723 26/10/35.
694 3/7/37.
4506 1/6/40.
1595 27/2/43.

SHEDS:
Brunswick 24/11/09.
Heaton Mersey 24/3/34.
Trafford Park 13/7/35.
Heaton Mersey 4/11/35.
Gorton 3/7/37.
Brunswick 2/6/38.
Trafford Park 16/9/39.
Chester 17/12/41.
Brunswick 31/7/43.

RENUMBERED:
5270 16/5/25.
2103 allocated.

CONDEMNED: 21/4/45.
Cut up at Gorton.

5862

Beyer, Peacock 3980.

To traffic 12/1898.

REPAIRS:
Gor. ?/?—25/5/12.**G.**
Superheated boiler fitted.
Gor. 17/6—2/9/22.**G.**
Gor. 31/1—27/6/25.**G.**
Gor. 29/10—17/12/27.**G.**
Gor. 24—31/3/28.**L.**
Gor. 15/6/29.**L.**

Gor. 28/12/29—1/2/30.**G.**
Gor. 10/10—14/11/31.**G.**
Gor. 19/5/33. *Not repaired.*

BOILERS:
436 *(new. sup.)* 25/5/12.
674 2/9/22.
519 27/6/25.
1723 14/11/31.

SHED:
Brunswick.

RENUMBERED:
5862 27/6/25.

CONDEMNED: 19/5/33.
Cut up at Gorton.

5863

Beyer, Peacock 3981.

To traffic 12/1898.

REPAIRS:
Gor. 22/2—18/4/08.**G.**
Gor. 30/6—11/8/10.**G.**
Gor. 11/10—20/12/19.**G.**
Superheated boiler fitted.
Gor. 1/10—17/12/21.**G.**
Gor. 26/4—12/7/24.**G.**
Gor. 25/9—18/12/26.**G.**
Gor. 7/7—18/8/28.**G.**
Gor. 24/5—5/7/30.**G.**
Gor. 9—23/7/32.**G.**
Gor. 14/4—12/5/34.**G.**
Gor. 20/7—10/8/35.**G.**

BOILERS:
260 18/4/08.
782 11/8/10.
1794 *(sup.)* 20/12/19.
746 18/8/28.
755 23/7/32.
694 12/5/34.

SHEDS:
Brunswick.
Trafford Park 25/7/32.
Brunswick 26/5/33.
Trafford Park 10/8/35.

RENUMBERED:
5863 12/7/24.

CONDEMNED: 30/4/37.
Into Gor. for cut up 1/5/37.

5864

Beyer, Peacock 3982.

To traffic 1/1899.

REPAIRS:
Gor. ?/?—29/6/12.**G.**
Superheated boiler fitted.
Gor. 26/8—14/10/22.**G.**
Gor. 31/1—18/4/25.**G.**
Gor. 22/10—3/12/27.**G.**
Gor. 2/11—14/12/29.**G.**
Gor. 5—26/3/32.**G.**
Gor. 2—16/9/33.**G.**
Gor. 20/7—10/8/35.**G.**
Gor. 5—26/12/36.**G.**
Gor. 25/9—2/10/37.**G.**
Gor. 11/10/38. *Not repaired.*

BOILERS:
637 *(sup.)* 29/6/12.
674 18/4/25.
1589 26/3/32.
1723 16/9/33.
288 10/8/35.
4510 26/12/36.

SHEDS:
Brunswick.
Trafford Park 10/8/35.
Gorton 27/12/36.
Heaton Mersey 2/5/37.

RENUMBERED:
5864 18/4/25.

CONDEMNED: 11/10/38.
Cut up at Gorton.

5865

Beyer, Peacock 3983.

To traffic 2/1899.

REPAIRS:
Gor. 5/4—29/5/09.**G.**
Gor. 16/9/11—18/5/12.**G.**
Superheated boiler fitted.
Gor. 4/12/20—8/1/21.**G.**
Gor. 1/9—1/12/23.**G.**
Gor. 23/8—27/9/24.**G.**
Gor. 27/3—12/6/26.**G.**
Gor. 28/4—16/6/28.**G.**
Gor. 31/8—19/10/29.**G.**
Gor. 24/10—28/11/31.**G.**
Gor. 16—30/12/33.**G.**
Gor. 31/8—21/9/35.**G.**
Gor. 6—20/2/37.**G.**
Gor. 31/12/38—21/1/39.**G.**
Gor. 6/10—1/11/41.**G.**
Gor. 11/2—25/3/44.**G.**
Gor. 23/12/44.**L.**

Gor. 26/5—23/6/45.**G.**

BOILERS:
948 29/5/09.
318 *(sup.)* 18/5/12.
480A 8/1/21.
742 16/6/28.
693 28/11/31.
742 30/12/33.
971 21/9/35.
4503 20/2/37.
693 21/1/39.
978 1/11/41.
973 25/3/44.

SHEDS:
Trafford Park 2/11/18.
Walton-on-the-Hill 16/2/28.
Brunswick 20/2/28.
Heaton Mersey 28/11/36.
Trafford Park 10/1/38.
Immingham 25/2/39.
Brunswick 18/3/40.
Northwich 12/11/41.
Brunswick 16/12/45.
Walton-on-the-Hill 5/5/46.
Northwich 14/7/46.

RENUMBERED:
865c 1/12/23.
5865 12/6/26.
2104 7/12/46.

CONDEMNED: 20/12/46.
Into Gor. for cut up 21/12/46.

5866

Beyer, Peacock 3984.

To traffic 2/1899.

REPAIRS:
Gor. 24/7—2/10/15.**G.**
Gor. 17/11—22/12/17.**G.**
Gor. 6/5—29/7/22.**G.**
Gor. 16/8—1/11/24.**G.**
Gor. 19/2—23/4/27.**G.**
Superheated boiler fitted.
Gor. 1/12/28—12/1/29.**G.**
Gor. 22/9/30. *Not repaired.*

BOILERS:
135 2/10/15.
586 22/12/17.
699 *(sup.)* 23/4/27.

SHEDS:
Trafford Park.
Walton-on-the-Hill 16/2/28.
Brunswick 20/2/28.

RENUMBERED:
5866 1/11/24.

5866 cont./
CONDEMNED: 22/9/30.
Cut up at Gorton.

5867

Beyer, Peacock 3985.

To traffic 2/1899.

REPAIRS:
Gor. 13/1—19/2/10.**G.**
Gor. 24/10—21/11/14.**G.**
Gor. 23/4—4/6/21.**G.**
Gor. 19/4—19/7/24.**G.**
Gor. 5—31/12/25.**L.**
Gor. 30/4—11/6/27.**G.**
Gor. 1/6—13/7/29.**G.**
Superheated boiler fitted.
Gor. 20/6—11/7/31.**G.**
Gor. 29/9/32. Not repaired.

BOILERS:
1165 19/2/10.
 737 21/11/14.
 586 11/6/27.
 171 (sup.) 13/7/29.
  89 11/7/31.

SHEDS:
Trafford Park.
Walton-on-the-Hill 16/2/28.
Brunswick 17/2/28.
Trafford Park 10/8/31.

RENUMBERED:
5867 19/7/24.

CONDEMNED: 29/9/32.
Cut up at Gorton.

5868

Beyer, Peacock 3986.

To traffic 2/1899.

REPAIRS:
Gor. 6/12/04—25/3/05.**G.**
Gor. 25/1—28/6/13.**G.**
Superheated boiler fitted.
Gor. 28/1—26/8/22.**G.**
Gor. 28/3—11/7/25.**G.**
Gor. 25/6—13/8/27.**G.**
Gor. 20/4—18/5/29.**G.**
Gor. 1/11—6/12/30.**G.**
Gor. 22/4/33. Not repaired.

BOILERS:
 204 25/3/05.
 171 (sup.) 28/6/13.
1794 18/5/29.
1563 6/12/30.

SHEDS:
Trafford Park at 4/22.
Brunswick by 3/29.

RENUMBERED:
5868 11/7/25.

CONDEMNED: 22/4/33.
Cut up at Gorton.

5869

Beyer, Peacock 3987.

To traffic 2/1899.

REPAIRS:
Gor. ?/?—16/2/07.**G.**
Gor. 7/2—18/4/14.**G.**
Superheated boiler fitted.
Gor. 15/7/22—27/1/23.**G.**
Gor. 30/5—8/8/25.**G.**
Gor. 12/11/27—7/1/28.**G.**
Gor. 30/11/29—11/1/30.**G.**
Gor. 20/2—5/3/32.**G.**
Gor. 30/12/33—27/1/34.**G.**
Westinghouse brake removed.
Gor. 4/1—8/2/36.**G.**
Gor. 5/6—10/7/37.**L.**
Gor. 9/4—7/5/38.**G.**
Gor. 20/7—3/8/40.**G.**
Gor. 11—21/2/42.**L.**

BOILERS:
 737 16/2/07.
 189 (sup.) 18/4/14.
 976 5/3/32.
 732 27/1/34.
 742 8/2/36.
 733 7/5/38.
 694 3/8/40.

SHED:
Brunswick 22/7/21.

RENUMBERED:
5869 8/8/25.

CONDEMNED: 14/6/43.
Into Gor. for cut up 26/6/43.

5870

Beyer, Peacock 3988.

To traffic 3/1899.

REPAIRS:
Gor. ?/?—27/7/12.**G.**
Superheated boiler fitted.
Gor. 28/8—16/10/20.**G.**
Gor. 29/9—8/12/23.**G.**
Gor. 22/11/24—28/3/25.**G.**
Gor. 4/2—17/3/28.**G.**
Gor. 5/10—16/11/29.**G.**
Gor. 27/6/31. Not repaired.

BOILERS:
480A (new. sup.) 27/7/12.
 172 16/10/20.
1623 28/3/25.

SHED:
Trafford Park.

RENUMBERED:
870c 8/12/23.
5870 28/3/25.

CONDEMNED: 27/6/31.
Cut up at Gorton.

5871

Beyer, Peacock 3989.

To traffic 3/1899.

REPAIRS:
Gor. ?/?—30/11/01.**G.**
Gor. 27/9—29/11/13.**G.**
Superheated boiler fitted.
Gor. 2/7—27/8/21.**G.**
Gor. 22/9—8/12/23.**G.**
Saturated boiler fitted.
Gor. 4/7—22/8/25.**G.**
Superheated boiler fitted.
Gor. 28/1—10/3/28.**G.**
Gor. 12/4—31/5/30.**G.**
Gor. 21/5—18/6/32.**G.**
Gor. 23/6—7/7/34.**G.**
Gor. 25/1—8/2/36.**G.**
Gor. 5—26/2/38.**G.**
Gor. 8—22/6/40.**G.**
Gor. 30/1—20/2/43.**G.**
Gor. 8—29/7/44.**G.**
Gor. 18/5/46. Not repaired.

BOILERS:
 251 30/11/01.
 519 (sup.) 29/11/13.
 456 (sat.) 8/12/23.
 637 (sup.) 22/8/25.
1840 18/6/32.
 755 7/7/34.
 660 8/2/36.
 732 26/2/38.
 369 22/6/40.
 978 29/7/44.

SHEDS:
Brunswick 14/5/20.
Walton-on-the-Hill 20/12/40.
Chester 3/1/43.
Brunswick 31/7/43.

RENUMBERED:
871c 8/12/23.
5871 22/8/25.
2105 allocated.

CONDEMNED: 14/6/46.
Cut up at Gorton.

5872

Beyer, Peacock 3990.

To traffic 3/1899.

REPAIRS:
Gor. 7/1—19/2/10.**G.**
Gor. 23/11/12—8/2/13.**G.**
Superheated boiler fitted.
Gor. 23/4—28/5/21.**G.**
Gor. 6/10/23—5/1/24.**G.**
Gor. 21/6—5/7/24.**L.**
Gor. 11/7—3/10/25.**G.**
Gor. 24/12/27—11/2/28.**G.**
Gor. 15/12/28—16/2/29.**G.**
Gor. 31/8—14/9/29.**G.**
Gor. 16/5—20/6/31.**G.**
Gor. 4/3/33. Not repaired.

BOILERS:
 977 19/2/10.
 904 (sup.) 8/2/13.
 318 28/5/21.
1595 14/9/29.
 909 20/6/31.

SHEDS:
Trafford Park.
Heaton Mersey 2/11/32.
Brunswick 4/2/33.

RENUMBERED:
872c 5/1/24.
5872 3/10/25.

CONDEMNED: 4/3/33.
Cut up at Gorton.

5873

Beyer, Peacock 3991.

To traffic 3/1899.

REPAIRS:
Gor. ?/?—1/2/13.**G.**
Superheated boiler fitted.
Gor. 28/8—20/11/20.**G.**
Gor. 21/10—18/11/22.**G.**
Gor. 22/11/24—24/1/25.**G.**
Gor. 31/12/26—5/3/27.**G.**
Gor. 5/5—23/6/28.**G.**
Gor. 30/6/30. Not repaired.

The class was not originally fitted with smokebox ash ejector, their fitting only starting in 1911. Ash ejectors fitted prior to 1920 had a short supply pipe, the steam entering the smokebox at the rear and this led to scouring of the front tube plate.

The steam entry point was moved further forward, a medium length pipe being put on engines which were not superheated.

Superheated engines had the steam entry point moved to the front of the smokebox, a longer external pipe being fitted. Gorton works.

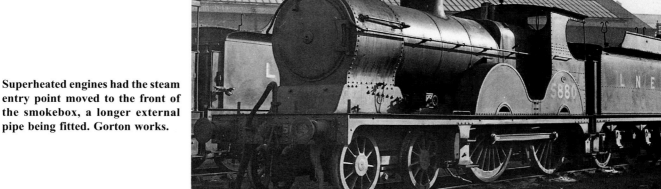

Most retained the ash ejector until withdrawal. No.2101 (ex5855) still had it in this April 1947 picture at Manchester (Central), and it was withdrawn in the following December. Note wheel and handle retained for smokebox door fastening but the top lamp iron has been moved to the front of the smokebox door.

The steam pipe to the ash ejector was normally on the left side of the smokebox but on the four engines with Westinghouse pump, 5857, 5859, 5869, 5876, it was located on the right side.

5873 cont./
BOILERS:
1081 *(new. sup.)* 1/2/13.
  782 20/11/20.
  743 23/6/28.

SHEDS:
Trafford Park *at* 4/22.
Brunswick *by* 3/29.

RENUMBERED:
5873 24/1/25.

CONDEMNED: 30/6/30.
Cut up at Gorton.

_____

5874

Beyer, Peacock 3992.

To traffic 3/1899.

REPAIRS:
Gor. 13/1—19/2/10.**G.**
Gor. 30/5—18/7/14.**G.**
Superheated boiler fitted.
Gor. 23/12/22—3/3/23.**G.**
Gor. 16/8—25/10/24.**G.**
Gor. 20/3—10/7/26.**G.**
Gor. 16/6—28/7/28.**G.**
Gor. 18/10—22/11/30.**G.**
Gor. 16—30/1/32.**L.**
Gor. 28/1—11/2/33.**G.**
Gor. 30/12/33—20/1/34.**G.**
Gor. 13—27/7/35.**G.**
Gor. 5—31/12/36.**G.**
Gor. 24/12/38—14/1/39.**G.**
Gor. 31/5—28/6/41.**G.**
Gor. 11—27/11/43.**G.**
Gor. 3—24/8/46.**G.**
Gor. 31/12/47. *Not repaired.*

BOILERS:
1117 19/2/10.
  297 *(sup.)* 18/7/14.
  690 10/7/26.
  688 11/2/33.
  741 20/1/34.
4506 27/7/35.
  979 31/12/36.
  973 14/1/39.
4514 27/11/43.
  279 24/8/46.

SHEDS:
Trafford Park 5/4/19.
Walton-on-the-Hill 18/2/28.
Brunswick 20/2/28.
Trafford Park 4/5/31.
Gorton 27/12/36.

Immingham 25/5/37.
Brunswick 18/3/40.
Northwich 25/8/46.
RENUMBERED:
5874 25/10/24.
2106 3/11/46

CONDEMNED: 31/12/47.
Cut up at Dukinfield.

_____

5875

Beyer, Peacock 3993.

To traffic 3/1899.

REPAIRS:
Gor. 15/6—31/7/09.**G.**
Gor. 7/12/12—15/2/13.**G.**
Superheated boiler fitted.
Gor. 20/12/19—6/3/20.**G.**
Gor. 28/1—25/2/22.**G.**
Gor. 12/7—18/10/24.**G.**
Gor. 13/2—24/4/26.**G.**
Gor. 12/5—23/6/28.**G.**
Gor. 31/5—19/7/30.**G.**
Gor. 1—29/10/32.**G.**
Gor. 21/4—12/5/34.**G.**

BOILERS:
  253 31/7/09.
  110 *(sup.)* 15/2/13.
1840 6/3/20.
  900 23/6/28.
  686 29/10/32.
  973 12/5/34.

SHEDS:
Trafford Park.
Walton-on-the-Hill 17/2/28.
Brunswick 20/2/28.

RENUMBERED:
5875 18/10/24.

CONDEMNED: 27/11/35.
Into Gor. for cut up 30/11/35.

_____

5876

Beyer, Peacock 3994.

To traffic 3/1899.

REPAIRS:
Gor. 15/2—21/3/08.**G.**
Gor. 23/9/10—14/1/11.**G.**
Gor. 11/1—29/3/13.**G.**
Superheated boiler fitted.

Gor. 25/10—20/12/19.**G.**
Gor. 13/5—2/9/22.**G.**
Gor. 1/12/23—9/2/24.**G.**
Gor. 12/12/25—6/3/26.**G.**
Gor. 26/11/27—14/1/28.**G.**
Gor. 23/11/29—18/1/30.**G.**
Gor. 20/6—11/7/31.**G.**
Gor. 3/9—29/10/32.**G.**
Westinghouse brake removed.
Gor. 30/9—14/10/33.**G.**
Gor. 20/4—11/5/35.**G.**
Gor. 27/3—24/4/37.**G.**
Gor. 27/11—4/12/37.**L.**
Gor. 14/3/39. *Not repaired.*

BOILERS:
  319 21/3/08.
1122 14/1/11.
  674 *(sup.)* 29/3/13.
1824 20/12/19.
  206 6/3/26.
  971 11/7/31.
  161 14/10/33.
  731 11/5/35.

SHEDS:
Trafford Park *at* 14/8/23.
Brunswick 11/5/35.

RENUMBERED:
5876 9/2/24.

CONDEMNED: 14/3/39.
Cut up at Gorton.

_____

5877

Beyer, Peacock 3995.

To traffic 3/1899.

REPAIRS:
Gor. 17/3—23/4/10.**G.**
Gor. 29/11—4/4/14.**G.**
Superheated boiler fitted.
Gor. 4/9—30/10/20.**G.**
Gor. 23/6—17/11/23.**G.**
Gor. 23/1—22/5/26.**G.**
Gor. 21/7—1/9/28.**G.**
Gor. 4/10—15/11/30.**G.**
Gor. 12/7/32. *Not repaired.*

BOILERS:
  686 23/4/10.
  62 *(sup.)* 4/4/14.
  688 22/5/26.

SHEDS:
Brunswick.
Trafford Park 25/1/32.

RENUMBERED:
  877c 17/11/23.
5877 22/5/26.

CONDEMNED: 12/7/32.
Cut up at Gorton.

_____

5878

Beyer, Peacock 3996

To traffic 3/1899.

REPAIRS:
Gor. 2/5—18/7/08.**G.**
Gor. 10/11—25/12/09.**G.**
Gor. 2/12/22—5/5/23.**G.**
Gor. 8/12/23—5/1/24.**L.**
Casualty.
Gor. 11/10—13/12/24.**G.**
Gor. 4/12/26—5/2/27.**G.**
Gor. 12/1—9/2/29.**G.**
Gor. 14/3—18/4/31.**G.**
Gor. 3—17/3/34.**G.**
Superheated boiler fitted.
Gor. 4/5—1/6/35.**G.**
Gor. 1—29/5/37.**G.**
Gor. 29/10/38. *Not repaired.*

BOILERS:
246 18/7/08.
132 25/12/09.
115 9/2/29.
693 *(sup.)* 17/3/34.
362 29/5/37.

SHEDS:
Brunswick. *at* 18/9/26.
Walton-on-the-Hill.
Brunswick 23/12/27.
Heaton Mersey 4/8/31.
Trafford Park 8/2/33.
Brunswick 7/7/33.

RENUMBERED:
5878 13/12/24.

CONDEMNED: 29/10/38.
Cut up at Gorton.

_____

5879

Beyer, Peacock 3997.

To traffic 4/1899.

REPAIRS:
Gor. 3/10—21/11/08.**G.**
Gor. 15/3—31/5/19.**G.**

WORKS CODES:- Bpk - Beyer, Peacock. Cow - Cowlairs. Dar- Darlington. Don - Doncaster. Efd - Eastfield. Ghd - Gateshead. Gor - Gorton. Inv - Inverurie. Str - Stratford. Wfd - Woodford.
REPAIR CODES:- **C/H** - Casual Heavy. **C/L** - Casual Light. **G** - General. **H**- Heavy. **H/I** - Heavy Intermediate. **L** - Light. **L/I** - Light Intermediate. **N/C** - Non-Classified.

5879 cont./
Superheated boiler fitted.
Gor. 5/3—9/4/21.**G.**
Gor. 19/5—7/7/23.**G.**
Gor. 6/2—10/4/26.**G.**
Gor. 23/6—21/7/28.**G.**
Gor. 15/11—20/12/30.**G.**
Gor. 4—18/3/33.**G.**
Gor. 3—17/11/34.**G.**
Gor. 21/3—11/4/36.**G.**
Gor. 25/9—9/10/37.**L.**
Gor. 18/6—9/7/38.**G.**
Gor. 23/11—7/12/40.**G.**
Gor. 28/10/43. *Not repaired.*

BOILERS:
1248 21/11/08.
 247 *(sup.)* 31/5/19.
1840 21/7/28.
 327 20/12/30.
 89 18/3/33.
 279 17/11/34.
 688 11/4/36.
 742 9/7/38.
4514 7/12/40.

SHED:
Brunswick.

RENUMBERED:
5879 10/4/26.
2107 allocated.

CONDEMNED: 20/11/43.
Cut up at Gorton.

5880

Beyer, Peacock 3998.

To traffic 4/1899.

REPAIRS:
Gor. ?/?—1/11/01.**G.**
Gor. 9/3—13/5/05.**G.**
Gor. 3/12/10—4/3/11.**G.**
Gor. 23/12/22—16/6/23.**G.**
Superheated boiler fitted.
Gor. 10/10/25—30/1/26.**G.**
Gor. 17/3—28/4/28.**G.**
Gor. 15/3—26/4/30.**G.**
Gor. 7—28/5/32.**G.**
Gor. 10—24/3/34.**G.**
Gor. 16/3—13/4/35.**G.**
Gor. 26/12/36—16/1/37.**G.**

BOILERS:
 238 1/11/01.
1122 13/5/05.
 456 4/3/11.
 436 *(sup.)* 16/6/23.
 661 30/1/26.
 362 24/3/34.
4506 16/1/37.

SHEDS:
Brunswick.
Trafford Park 6/5/35.
Heaton Mersey 29/10/35.
Gorton 27/12/36.
Immingham 25/5/37.

RENUMBERED:
5880 30/1/26.

CONDEMNED: 21/4/39.
Into Gor. for cut up 22/4/39.

5881

Beyer, Peacock 3999.

To traffic 4/1899.

REPAIRS:
Gor. 2/3—29/4/05.**G.**
Gor. 19/10—21/12/12.**G.**
Superheated boiler fitted.
Gor. 22/11/19—24/1/20.**G.**
Gor. 10/3—28/7/23.**G.**
Gor. 20/3—31/7/26.**G.**
Gor. 18/8—29/9/28.**G.**
Gor. 7/2—7/3/31.**G.**
Gor. 8/12/32. *Not repaired.*

BOILERS:
 282 .
1119 29/4/05.
 699 *(sup.)* 21/12/12.
 691 31/7/26.

SHED:
Brunswick.

RENUMBERED:
5881 31/7/26.

CONDEMNED: 8/12/32.
Cut up at Gorton.

(below) **All had steam sanding, but only to the leading coupled wheels. For running in reverse, gravity sanding could be applied from boxes on the front of the tender. Trafford Park.**

(above) All were provided with the standard tender holding 6 tons of coal and 4000 gallons of water, but after being superseded on the London Extension, at least five, Nos.868, 871, 872, 874 and 875, changed to the 3080 gallon type. By Grouping all except No.871 had 4000 gallon tender and that engine had one again from December 1923. The standard 4000 gallon tender had copings with ends flared and a half round beading to the edge. Only from 1924 were steps added to the rear end.

(centre) As their work did not need water pick-up apparatus, they could use the 4000 gallon tenders of J10 class goods engines. These could be identified because their copings had straight ends and no beading. This type were coupled to seven D6's: 5268 (6/31-7/33), 5853 (1/38-5/39), 5855 (9/39-12/47), 5863 (7/32-4/37), 5871 (6/40-6/46), 5874 (8/46-12/47), 5878 (7/35-10/38).

No.869 at Manchester (Central) in early LNER days. This was one of the four D6's to acquire Westinghouse brake for working the GER stock of the Harwich-Liverpool boat trains. From 1927 B12's took over this duty and the Westinghouse equipment became redundant, however, it was not removed for some years, No.869 keeping it until 'shopped' in January 1934.

Six similar engines, Nos.562 to 567 were built by Gorton in 1890. These had deeper framing, buffers with parallel shanks, and deeper footsteps. By Grouping they had all been fitted with Belpaire firebox, Robinson chimney, and extended cab roof. They also had a casing to the Ramsbottom safety valves. Doncaster.

Between November 1891 and May 1892, Gorton built six more, Nos.682 to 687, to the same design and details. The same cab, boiler, and chimney modifications to them were made before Grouping.

Twelve more, Nos.700 to 711, to the Gorton specification, were built by Kitson in 1892. They also underwent the same cab, boiler and chimney changes whilst still in GCR ownership. The class reached a total of thirty-one in 1894 when a final batch of six, Nos.688 to 693 were built at Gorton.

CLASS D 7

5561

Kitson & Co. 3010.

To traffic 11/1887.

REPAIRS:
Gor. 12/8—23/12/16.**G.**
Reb. with Standard No.1 boiler.
Gor. 24/7—23/10/20.**G.**
Gor. 24/2—2/6/23.**G.**
Gor. 3/7—16/10/26.**G.**
Gor. 17/9/28. *Not repaired.*

BOILERS:
1654 23/12/16.
 623 16/10/26.

SHED:
Immingham.

RENUMBERED:
5561 16/10/26.

CONDEMNED: 17/9/28.
Cut up at Gorton.

────────────

5562

Gorton.

To traffic 4/1890.

REPAIRS:
Gor. 12/6—8/8/08.**G.**
Gor. 23/11—21/12/12.**G.**
Reb. with Standard No.1 boiler.
Gor. 7/5—24/9/21.**G.**
Gor. 19/4—5/7/24.**G.**
Gor. 18/6—27/8/27.**G.**
Gor. 24/9—1/10/27.**L.**
Casualty.
Gor. 31/5—5/7/30.**G.**
Gor. 17—31/12/32.**G.**

BOILERS:
 596 8/8/08.
 227 21/12/12.
1695 27/8/27.
 241 31/12/32.

SHEDS:
Lincoln GC. *at* 4/22.
Mexborough *by* 1925.
Immingham 2/11/33.
New Holland 28/11/34.

RENUMBERED:
5562 5/7/24.

CONDEMNED: 22/8/35 .
Into Gor. for cut up 24/8/35.

────────────

5563

Gorton .

To traffic 4/1890.

REPAIRS:
Gor. ?/?—?5/10.**G.**
Reb. with Standard No.1 boiler.
Gor. 3/4—15/5/15.**G.**
Gor. 11/2—29/4/22.**G.**
Gor. 10/5—9/8/24.**G.**
Gor. 14/8/26—8/1/27.**G.**
Gor. 12—19/2/27.**L.**
Wheels only.
Gor. 5/10/29. *Not repaired.*

BOILERS:
1123 15/5/15.
 526 9/8/24.

SHED:
Mexborough.

RENUMBERED:
5563 9/8/24.

CONDEMNED: 5/10/29.
Cut up at Gorton.

────────────

5564

Gorton.

To traffic 7/1890.

REPAIRS:
Gor. ?/?—?/7/10.**G.**
Reb. with Standard No.1 boiler.
Gor. 15/5—17/7/15.**G.**
Gor. 5/3—9/4/21.**G.**
Gor. 3/11/23—5/1/24.**G.**
Gor. 23/10/26. *Not repaired.*

BOILERS:
 219 17/7/15.
1742 5/1/24.

SHED:
Lincoln GC.

RENUMBERED:
564c ?/2/24.
5564 5/1/24.

CONDEMNED: 14/12/26.
Cut up at Gorton.

────────────

5565

Gorton.

To traffic 8/1890.

REPAIRS:
Gor. 4/8—25/9/09.**G.**
Gor. 12/8—4/11/11.**G.**
Reb. with Standard No.1 boiler.
Gor. 28/5—16/7/21.**G.**
Gor. 24/5—4/10/24.**G.**
Gor. 5/11—10/12/27.**G.**
Gor. 28/6—2/8/30.**G.**
Gor. 12/4/33. *Not repaired.*

BOILERS:
 199 25/9/09.
  44 4/11/11.
1750 4/10/24.
 159 2/8/30.

SHEDS:
Sheffield.
Mexborough 18/3/26.

RENUMBERED:
5565 4/10/24.

CONDEMNED: 12/4/33.
Cut up at Gorton.

────────────

5566

Gorton.

To traffic 9/1890.

REPAIRS:
Gor. 30/10/15—12/2/16.**G.**
Reb. with Standard No.1 boiler.
Gor. 25/11/22—10/2/23.**G.**
Gor. 3/10—5/12/25.**G.**
Gor. 22/1—26/3/27.**G.**
Gor. 11/5—22/6/29.**G.**
Gor. 19/8/31. *Not repaired.*

BOILERS:
1355 12/2/16.
1231 5/12/25.

SHED:
Immingham.

RENUMBERED:
5566 5/12/25.

CONDEMNED: 19/8/31.
Cut up at Gorton.

────────────

5567

Gorton.

To traffic 12/1890.

REPAIRS:
Gor. 5/6—10/7/15.**G.**
Gor. 16/3—1/6/18.**G.**
Reb. with Standard No.1 boiler.
Gor. 23/10—4/12/20.**G.**
Gor. 3/2—19/5/23.**G.**
Gor. 25/4—18/7/25.**G.**
Gor. 14/5—30/6/27.**G.**
Gor. 20/7—24/8/29.**G.**
Gor. 24/9/31. *Not repaired.*

BOILERS:
392 10/7/15.
667 1/6/18.
243 19/5/23.
167 30/6/27.
144 24/8/29.

SHEDS:
Immingham.
Barnsley 23/1/30.
Immingham 30/10/30.

RENUMBERED:
5567 18/7/25.

CONDEMNED: 24/9/31.
Cut up at Gorton.

────────────

5682

Gorton.

To traffic 11/1891.

REPAIRS:
Gor. ?/?—?/6/09.G.
Reb. with Standard No.1 boiler.
Gor. 10/4—21/8/15.**G.**
Gor. 27/11/20—19/3/21.**G.**
Gor. 6/10—8/12/23.**G.**
Gor. 15/8—7/11/25.**G.**
Gor. 18/6—6/8/27.**G.**
Gor. 21/9—19/10/29.**G.**
Gor. 31/12/31. *Not repaired.*

BOILERS:
1386 21/8/15.
 477 19/3/21.
1070 7/11/25.

No.5561 received a change of boiler in October 1926 and then got a casing around its safety valves. It also changed to parallel shank front buffers. The Robinson chimney was retained as were the twin handles for the smokebox door fastening. Its tender was the only one to which rear end footsteps were not fitted after Grouping.

Beginning with No.5710 on 29th March 1924, a slightly shorter 'plantpot' type chimney was fitted. This brought the height from rail level to 12ft 11^3/$_4$ in. but the dome height remained at 13ft 0^1/$_2$ in. and no attempt was made to bring the class within the 13ft 0in. load gauge. The chimney change on No.5706 was effective from 15th August 1925.

The majority got the chimney change whilst they still had the number on the tender, i.e. by 1929. No.5690 had its number put on the cab in May 1929, and was unusual in keeping the Robinson chimney. It did not go to works again until February 1934, when the chimney was changed to 'plantpot' type. (*see* page 34). The final batch had coil springs in place of leaf type for the driving wheels.

Until after 1930 it was usual for the safety valves to be enclosed in a rectangular casing, which was painted the same colour as the engine.

When changed to black in July 1930, No.5562 kept the safety valve casing.

This engine had one more repair - ex works 31st December 1932 - during which it got a newly built boiler, and this did not have a safety valve casing.

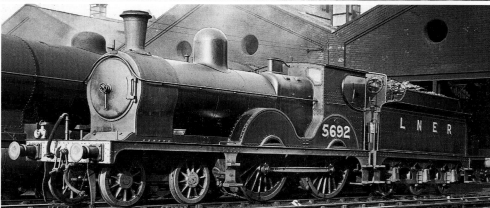

The original boilers had a round top firebox, but between June 1909 and June 1918 all thirty-one of the class had been changed to the GCR No.1 design standard boiler. This had a Belpaire firebox with two washout plugs and two handholes on the shoulder. Mexborough shed.

5682 cont./
167 19/10/29.

SHEDS:
Immingham.
New Holland.
Immingham 10/9/29
New Holland 20/11/29
Immingham.

RENUMBERED:
 682c 8/12/23.
5682 7/11/25.

CONDEMNED: 31/12/31.
Cut up at Gorton.

_____

5683

Gorton.

To traffic 12/1891.

REPAIRS:
Gor. ?/?—10/8/12.**G.**
Gor. 17/2—27/10/17.**G.**
Reb. with Standard No.1 boiler.
Gor. 29/11/19—20/3/20.**G.**
Gor. 12/8—14/10/22.**G.**
Gor. 31/1—16/5/25.**G.**
Gor. 12/11/27—7/1/28.**G.**
Gor. 22/3—26/4/30.**G.**
Gor. 23/7—13/8/32.**G.**
Gor. 7—14/7/34.**G.**
Gor. 25/8—22/9/34.**L.**

BOILERS:
 276 10/8/12.
1700 27/10/17.
 211 20/3/20.
 282 7/1/28.
 398 13/8/32.
 473 14/7/34.

SHEDS:
Sheffield.
Immingham 17/3/26.
New Holland 10/9/32.
Immingham 26/11/34.
New Holland 9/8/35.

RENUMBERED:
5683 16/5/25.

CONDEMNED: 10/4/37.
Into Don. for cut up 17/4/37.

_____

5684

Gorton.

To traffic 11/1891.

REPAIRS:
Gor. ?/?—2/3/01.**G.**
Gor. 4/2—23/3/07.**G.**
Gor. 16/2—18/5/12.**G.**
Reb. with Standard No.1 boiler.
Gor. 29/11/19—10/4/20.**G.**
Gor. 5/5—16/6/23.**G.**
Gor. 19/12/25—13/3/26.**G.**
Gor. 31/3—19/5/28.**G.**
Gor. 10/5—7/6/30.**G.**
Gor. 1—15/10/32.**G.**
Gor. 11/8—1/9/34.**G.**
Gor. 7—21/8/37.**G.**
Gor. 16/6/39. *Not repaired.*

BOILERS:
 595 2/3/01.
 276 23/3/07.
 480 18/5/12.
1695 10/4/20.
 119 13/3/26.
 215 7/6/30.
1778 15/10/32.
 188 1/9/34.
 758 21/8/37.

SHEDS:
New Holland.
Louth 14/7/30.
Immingham 8/7/32.
New Holland 28/12/32.
Immingham 26/11/34.
New Holland 13/9/35.

RENUMBERED:
5684 13/3/26.

CONDEMNED: 16/6/39.
Cut up at Gorton.

_____

5685

Gorton.

To traffic 1/1892.

REPAIRS:
Gor. ?/?—?/1/10.**G.**
Reb. with Standard No.1 boiler.
Gor. 2/10—13/11/15.**G.**
Gor. 27/7—7/12/18.**G.**
Gor. 19/11/21—18/2/22.**G.**
Gor. 8/3—31/5/24.**G.**
Gor. 4/9—27/11/26.**G.**

Gor. 27/10—8/12/28.**G.**
Gor. 4/7/30. *Not repaired.*

BOILERS:
 204 13/11/15.
 696 31/5/24.
1715 27/11/26.
  93 8/12/28.

SHEDS:
Immingham.
New Holland 16/9/29.
Immingham 22/1/30.

RENUMBERED:
5685 28/6/24.

CONDEMNED: 4/7/30.
Cut up at Gorton.

_____

5686

Gorton.

To traffic 3/1892.

REPAIRS:
Gor. 20/1—9/4/10.**G.**
Reb. with Standard No.1 boiler.
Gor. 24/10/14—6/2/15.**G.**
Gor. 24/11/17—6/4/18.**G.**
Gor. 14/1—6/5/22.**G.**
Gor. 21/6—9/8/24.**G.**
Gor. 31/12/26—5/3/27.**G.**
Gor. 24/11/28—12/1/29.**G.**
Gor. 21/3—25/4/31.**G.**
Gor. 28/8/33. *Not repaired.*

BOILERS:
 765 9/4/10.
 387 6/2/15.
 207 6/4/18.
 282 6/5/22.
1654 5/3/27.
 100 25/4/31.

SHEDS:
Immingham *at* 22/5/27.
New Holland.
Immingham 14/11/30.

RENUMBERED:
5686 9/8/24.

CONDEMNED: 28/8/33.
Cut up at Gorton.

_____

5687

Gorton.

To traffic 5/1892.

REPAIRS:
Gor. ?/?—3/5/02.**G.**
Gor. 10/4—26/6/09.**G.**
Reb. with Standard No.1 boiler.
Gor. 24/8—7/12/18.**G.**
Gor. 4/11/22—24/2/23.**G.**
Gor. 23/8—8/11/24.**G.**
Gor. 25/9—11/12/26.**G.**
Gor. 2/3—6/4/29.**G.**
Gor. 23/5—20/6/31.**G.**
Gor. 11—25/3/33.**G.**

BOILERS:
 391 3/5/02.
 735 26/6/09.
1767 7/12/18.
 287 11/12/26.
1641 20/6/31.
 211 25/3/33.

SHEDS:
Immingham.
New Holland 13/5/29.
Immingham.
New Holland 28/7/31.
Immingham 28/12/32.
New Holland 28/4/33.
Immingham 24/7/34.

RENUMBERED:
5687 8/11/24.

CONDEMNED: 22/8/35.
Into Don. for cut up 24/8/35.

_____

5688

Gorton.

To traffic 4/1894.

REPAIRS:
Gor. 8/7—9/12/16.**G.**
Reb. with Standard No.1 boiler.
Gor. 18/9—27/11/20.**G.**
Gor. 13/1—5/5/23.**G.**
Gor. 5/12/25—27/2/26.**G.**
Gor. 27/10—8/12/28.**G.**
Gor. 20/4/31. *Not repaired.*

BOILERS:
 109 9/12/16.
 942 5/5/23.
1641 8/12/28.

WORKS CODES:- Bpk - Beyer, Peacock. Cow - Cowlairs. Dar- Darlington. Don - Doncaster. Efd - Eastfield. Ghd - Gateshead. Gor - Gorton. Inv - Inverurie. Str - Stratford. Wfd - Woodford.
REPAIR CODES:- **C/H** - Casual Heavy. **C/L** - Casual Light. **G** - General. **H**- Heavy. **H/I** - Heavy Intermediate. **L** - Light. **L/I** - Light Intermediate. **N/C** - Non-Classified.

32

There were also two plugs and two handholes on the other side, at staggered positions. Frodingham shed.

Normal fastening for the smokebox door was by wheel and handle, although twin handles were noted on Nos.5561, 5564, 5565, 5682, 5691, 5700 and 5705.

On the engine there was steam sanding to the front of the leading coupled wheels only, the filler was through the running plate to boxes behind the footsteps.

For running in reverse, gravity sanding was available from boxes at the front end of the tender at footplate level.

Most of the class were equipped with carriage heating connection at both ends, many having the front end facility from before Grouping (*see* page 28).

The standard tender was the Parker design with a water capacity of 3080 gallons. From about 1910 solid coal guards were added and these had curved ends with a beading around the edge. After the LNER took over, much of their work involved tender-first running, so a weatherboard with lookout glasses was put on the tender. As shown in the illustration of No.5690 above, three short coal rails at each side were added between the coping and weatherboard.

5688 cont./
SHEDS:
Mexborough.
Immingham 18/3/30.

RENUMBERED:
5688 27/2/26.

CONDEMNED: 20/4/31.
Cut up at Gorton.

5689

Gorton.

To traffic 5/1894.

REPAIRS:
Gor. ?/?—28/9/02.**G.**
Gor. 15/8—24/10/08.**G.**
Gor. 5/5—12/8/11.**G.**
Reb. with Standard No.1 boiler.
Gor. 28/5—16/7/21.**G.**
Gor. 22/12/23—29/3/24.**G.**
Gor. 12/2—9/4/27.**G.**
Gor. 1—29/3/30.**G.**
Gor. 11—25/3/33.**G.**

BOILERS:
202 28/8/02.
974 24/10/08.
212 12/8/11.
261 16/7/21.
387 9/4/27.
104 29/3/30.
82 25/3/33.

SHEDS:
Mexborough.
Immingham 1/4/30.
New Holland 7/6/35.

RENUMBERED:
5689 19/4/24.

CONDEMNED: 13/2/36.
Into Don. for cut up 22/2/36.

5690

Gorton.

To traffic 5/1894.

REPAIRS:
Gor. ?/?—18/6/10.**G.**
Reb. with Standard No.1 boiler.
Gor. 26/2—18/6/21.**G.**
Gor. 11/8—6/10/23.**G.**
Gor. 24/7—31/12/26.**G.**
Gor. 13/4—11/5/29.**G.**
Gor. 24/2—10/3/34.**G.**

BOILERS:
678 18/6/10.
437 18/6/21.
124 31/12/26.
315 10/3/34.

SHEDS:
Mexborough.
Immingham 22/2/37.

RENUMBERED:
690c 6/10/23.
5690 31/12/26.

CONDEMNED: 22/5/37.
Into Don. for cut up 22/5/37.

5691

Gorton.

To traffic 7/1894.

REPAIRS:
Gor. 15/11—20/12/13.**G.**
Gor. 2/2—8/6/18.**G.**
Reb. with Standard No.1 boiler.
Gor. 15/5—16/10/20.**G.**
Gor. 2/6—21/7/23.**G.**
Gor. 22/5—31/7/26.**G.**
Gor. 9/2—16/3/29.**G.**
Gor. 19/7/33. *Not repaired.*

BOILERS:
202 20/12/13.
387 8/6/18.
83 31/7/26.

SHED:
Mexborough.

RENUMBERED:
5691 31/7/26.

CONDEMNED: 19/7/33.
Cut up at Gorton.

5692

Gorton.

To traffic 8/1894.

REPAIRS:
Gor. 31/7—23/10/09.**G.**
Gor. 8/6—20/7/12.**G.**
Gor. 16/1—27/3/15.**G.**
Reb. with Standard No.1 boiler.
Gor. 17/1—12/6/20.**G.**
Gor. 6/1—10/2/23.**G.**
Gor. 29/8—28/11/25.**G.**
Gor. 19/5—30/6/28.**G.**
Gor. 6/12/30—17/1/31.**G.**
Gor. 14—21/10/33.**G.**

BOILERS:
391 23/10/09.
1044 27/3/15.
1635 30/6/28.
459 21/10/33.

SHEDS:
Mexborough.
Immingham 4/9/36.

RENUMBERED:
5692 28/11/25.

CONDEMNED: 10/4/37.
Into Don. for cut up 17/4/37.

5693

Gorton.

To traffic 9/1894.

REPAIRS:
Gor. ?/?—?/5/12.**G.**
Reb. with Standard No.1 boiler.
Gor. 5/12/14—30/1/15.**G.**
Gor. 1/5—2/10/20.**G.**
Gor. 14/7—25/8/23.**G.**
Gor. 10/10—26/12/25.**G.**
Gor. 18/2—24/3/28.**G.**
Gor. 13/2/30. *Not repaired.*

BOILERS:
493 30/1/15.
1094 2/10/20.
1670 24/3/28.

SHEDS:
Sheffield.
Immingham 2/7/26.

RENUMBERED:
693c 29/9/23.
5693 26/12/25.

CONDEMNED: 13/2/30.
Cut up at Gorton.

5700

Kitson & Co. 3440.

To traffic 10/1892.

REPAIRS:
Gor. 26/1—27/2/09.**G.**
Gor. 29/12/11—17/2/12.**G.**
*Possibly reb. with Standard
No.1 boiler.*
Gor. 11/12/20—29/1/21.**G.**
Gor. 7/4—19/5/23.**G.**
Gor. 16/1—27/3/26.**G.**
Gor. 31/3—19/5/28.**G.**
Gor. 2/8—20/9/30.**G.**
Gor. 22/10—12/11/32.**G.**
Westinghouse pump removed.

BOILERS:
126 27/2/09.
147 17/2/12.
53 29/1/21.
477 27/3/26.
1655 20/9/30.
215 12/11/32.

SHEDS:
Lincoln.
New Holland 30/8/33.
Immingham 18/10/33.
New Holland 13/7/35.

RENUMBERED:
5700 27/3/26.

CONDEMNED: 16/5/36.
Into Don. for cut up 16/5/36.

5701

Kitson & Co. 3441.

To traffic 10/1892.

REPAIRS:
Gor. 21/3—2/5/08.**G.**
Gor. 1/3—7/6/13.**G.**
Reb. with Standard No.1 boiler.
Gor. 15/5—7/8/20.**G.**
Gor. 24/2—23/6/23.**G.**
Gor. 7/8—2310/26.**G.**
Gor. 20/10—8/12/28.**G.**
Gor. 6/9—18/10/30.**G.**
Gor. 12—26/8/33.**G.**

BOILERS:
394 2/5/08.
169 7/6/13.
213 23/10/26.
1044 8/12/28.
1764 26/8/33.

SHEDS:
Northwich.
Immingham 17/10/30.
New Holland 8/11/30.
Louth 12/1/32.
Immingham 30/8/32.
New Holland 26/11/34.

RENUMBERED:
5701 23/10/26.

CONDEMNED: 2/11/35.
Into Don. for cut up 2/11/35.

Although there were some exchanges, all except three retained tenders which had been built for this class. Nos.5703 (11/30 to 3/33), 5704 (from 3/33) and 5708 (from 12/33) did however run with tenders taken from J10 class engines but still of 3080 gallons capacity. The tender shown was put with No.5703 and then 5704 from March 1933 to October 1936. It was T5695 and had coping with curved ends but no beading (*see* also Appendix volume..

The above tender was condemned in October 1936 and engine 5704 then acquired the tender from J10 No.5080 which had a coping with square ends. In November 1933, a similar tender from J10 No.5090 had been coupled to D7 class 5708.

All the class had the vacuum brake for engine and train working, with ejector exhaust pipe through the boiler. In 1902/3, two engines, Nos.(5)700 and (5)705, were also fitted with Westinghouse brake for train working to deal with arrivals from the NER and GER. 705 appears here on the rather cramped yard at Sheffield Neepsend shed.

The extra Westinghouse brake was taken off No.5700 in November 1932 but No.5705 kept it to withdrawal in August 1933.

(right) Intended mainly for working passenger trains, they had the standard green, fully lined painting, with company arms on the leading splasher and on the tender.

(below) Possibly as an experiment, No.705 ran with a larger size of arms on the splasher but with company name only on the tender. No.705 is seen at Guide Bridge, probably running-in after shopping at Gorton.

5702

Kitson & Co. 3442.

To traffic 10/1892.

REPAIRS:
Gor. ?/?—?/7/09.**G.**
Reb. with Standard No.1 boiler.
Gor. 5—26/2/16.**G.**
Gor. 24/1—24/4/20.**G.**
Gor. 4/2—25/3/22.**G.**
Gor. 2/2—5/4/24.**G.**
Gor. 10/4—24/7/26.**G.**
Gor. 5/1—23/2/29.**G.**
Gor. 7—28/11/31.**G.**
Gor. 19/9/33. *Not repaired.*

BOILERS:
1340 26/2/16.
 480 24/4/20.
 170 24/7/26.
 965 28/11/31.

SHEDS:
Northwich.
Immingham 19/7/30.

RENUMBERED:
5702 24/5/24.

CONDEMNED: 19/9/33.
Cut up at Gorton.

_____

5703

Kitson & Co. 3443.

To traffic 10/1892.

REPAIRS:
Gor. 8/5—17/7/09.**G.**
Reb. with Standard No.1 boiler.
Gor. 11/1—2/8/19.**G.**
Gor. 16/4—4/6/21.**G.**
Gor. 27/1—21/4/23.**G.**
Gor. 13/6—29/8/25.**G.**
Gor. 3/12/27—21/1/28.**G.**
Gor. 26/4—31/5/30.**G.**
Gor. 8—29/11/30.**G.**
Gor. 4—18/3/33.**G.**

BOILERS:
528 17/7/09.
119 2/8/19.
215 29/8/25.
 14 31/5/30.
180 18/3/33.

SHEDS:
Northwich.
Immingham 6/4/26.
Louth 11/7/32.
Immingham 15/10/32.

Louth 28/4/33.
New Holland 18/10/33.

RENUMBERED:
5703 29/8/25.

CONDEMNED: 29/5/35.
Into Don. for cut up 1/6/35.

_____

5704

Kitson & Co. 3444.

To traffic 11/1892.

REPAIRS:
Gor. ?/?—21/12/07.**G.**
Gor. 26/10/12—4/1/13.**G.**
Reb. with Standard No.1 boiler.
Gor. 29/1—5/3/21.**G.**
Gor. 28/4—2/6/23.**G.**
Gor. 22/11/24—17/1/25.**G.**
Gor. 15/10—26/11/27.**G.**
Gor. 31/12/29—8/2/30.**G.**
Gor. 4—18/3/33.**G.**
Gor. 31/10—7/11/36.**G.**
Gor. 23/12/39. *Not repaired.*

BOILERS:
1347 21/12/07.
 795 4/1/13.
  85 5/3/21.
1897 26/11/27.
  79 8/2/30.
 902 18/3/33.
 496 7/11/36.

SHEDS:
Northwich.
Mexborough 15/5/30.
Immingham 15/8/33.
Frodingham 10/7/35.
New Holland 22/4/37.
Immingham 31/3/39.

RENUMBERED:
5704 17/1/25.

CONDEMNED: 23/12/39.
Cut up at Doncaster 4/40.

_____

5705

Kitson & Co. 3445.

To traffic 11/1892.

REPAIRS:
Gor. 2/5—6/6/08.**L.**
Gor. 21/10/10—17/2/11.**G.**
Reb. with Standard No.1 boiler.
Gor. 3/2—29/7/17.**G.**
Gor. 6/3/20—22/1/21.**G.**

Gor. 21/7—13/10/23.**G.**
Gor. 3/7—18/9/26.**G.**
Gor. 16/2—6/4/29.**G.**
Gor. 28/3—2/5/31.**G.**
Gor. 1/8/33. *Not repaired.*

BOILERS:
 632 6/6/08.
 659 17/2/11.
1690 29/7/17.
1715 22/1/21.
 382 18/9/26.
 459 2/5/31.

SHEDS:
Lincoln.
New Holland 27/2/32.
Immingham 18/7/32.

RENUMBERED:
 705c 13/10/23.
5705 18/9/26.

CONDEMNED: 1/8/33.
Cut up at Gorton.

_____

5706

Kitson & Co. 3446.

To traffic 11/1892.

REPAIRS:
Gor. 25/8—16/10/09.**G.**
Gor. 14/10—9/12/11.**G.**
Reb. with Standard No.1 boiler.
Gor. 5/2—12/3/21.**G.**
Gor. 18/8—10/11/23.**G.**
Gor. 23/5—15/8/25.**G.**
Gor. 29/10—31/12/27.**G.**
Gor. 5/4—3/5/30.**G.**
Gor. 9—30/8/30.**L.**
After collision.
Gor. 28/5—11/6/32.**G.**

BOILERS:
 110 16/10/09.
 767 9/12/11.
  92 12/3/21.
1670 15/8/25.
 261 31/12/27.
1343 11/6/32.

SHEDS:
New Holland.
Immingham 28/2/30.
New Holland.
Immingham 27/2/32.
New Holland 27/6/32.
Immingham 29/1/34.
New Holland 6/4/35.
Immingham 7/6/35.

RENUMBERED:
 706c 10/11/23.
5706 15/8/25.

CONDEMNED: 2/8/35.
Into Don. for cut up 10/8/35.

_____

5707

Kitson & Co. 3447.

To traffic 11/1892.

REPAIRS:
Gor. 22/4—26/6/09.**G.**
Reb. with Standard No.1 boiler.
Gor. 22/5—16/10/20.**G.**
Gor. 18/2—1/4/22.**G.**
Gor. 10/2—17/3/23.**G.**
Gor. 24/1—4/4/25.**G.**
Gor. 22/5—21/8/26.**G.**
Gor. 1/12/28—9/2/29.**G.**
Gor. 18/4—16/5/31.**G.**
Gor. 19/5/33. *Not repaired.*

BOILERS:
970 26/6/09.
314 16/10/20.
692 9/2/29.

SHEDS:
Northwich.
Immingham 2/6/30.

RENUMBERED:
5707 4/4/25.

CONDEMNED: 19/5/33.
Cut up at Gorton.

_____

5708

Kitson & Co. 3448.

To traffic 11/1892.

REPAIRS:
Gor. ?/?—1/2/08.**G.**
Gor. 10/7—16/10/15.**G.**
Reb. with Standard No.1 boiler.
Gor. 6/11/20—26/2/21.**G.**
Gor. 22/9—22/12/23.**G.**
Gor. 2/1—10/4/26.**G.**
Gor. 8/10—3/12/27.**G.**
Gor. 22/2—22/3/30.**G.**
Gor. 9—23/12/33.**G.**

BOILERS:
1355 1/2/08.
1579 16/10/15.
  83 26/2/21.
 928 10/4/26.
 306 23/12/33.

No.709, ex paint shop 3rd March 1923, was the first D7 in Group painting. The engine kept its GC brass numberplate and arms on the splasher but the tender changed to L. & N. E. R. above the number which it now also carried. To 2nd June 1923, Nos.566, 687, 692, 703 and 707 also got this style but without the GC coat of arms.

When Nos.688 and 700 were ex paint shop on 30th June 1923, the full points and the ampersand had been discarded and only LNER was used thereafter. Nos.561, 567, 684, 688, 691, 700, 701 and 704 got that style, to which, from 29th September 1923 on No.693 the suffix C was added to the number. To 29th December 1923 Nos.682, 690, 693, 705, 706 and 708 also got the suffix. No.564, ex paint shop 19th January 1924, was also recorded as having suffix but made no further visit to works.

The change to the 1924 LNER numbering began with No.5711, ex paint shop 2nd February 1924. That one, and 5689 (19/4/24), 5710 (17/5/24) and 5702 (24/5/24), were also fitted with GC type plates bearing those numbers. Sheffield (Victoria).

The use of GCR details ceased when No.5685 was ex paint shop on 28th June 1924. On its cab it had the Group Standard 8⅝in. number plate. This photograph shows the uniform livery which all the class then acquired until the June 1928 economies became applicable.

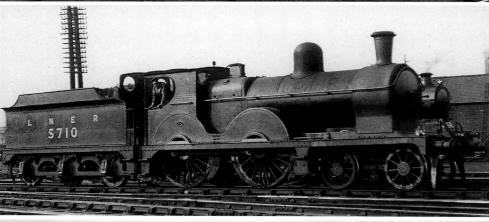

The change to black paint with single red lining began with Nos.5692 (30/6/28) and 5710 (7/7/28) and until May 1929 the number remained on the tender. Nos.5685, 5686, 5687, 5688, 5691, 5692, 5701, 5702, 5705, 5707 and 5710 were painted in this guise.

The final livery, effective from 11th May 1929, had the number inside the rear splasher beading, the plate being moved up slightly to accommodate the 12in. figures. The tender lettering became 12in. instead of 7½ in. but (curiously) remained on the same level instead of centred on the panel. This was to clear the horizontal row of rivet heads at the centre. Gorton works.

5708 cont./
SHEDS:
Immingham.
Northwich 6/4/26.
Mexborough 16/5/30.
Frodingham 14/9/36.

RENUMBERED:
708c 22/12/23.
5708 10/4/26.

CONDEMNED: 25/5/37.
Into Don. for cut up 25/5/37.

_____

5709

Kitson & Co. 3449.

To traffic 11/1892.

REPAIRS:
Gor. ?/?—?/1/11.**G.**
Reb. with Standard No.1 boiler.
Gor. 31/10—28/11/14.**G.**
Gor. 10/1—24/7/20.**G.**
Gor. 18/11/22—13/1/23.**G.**
Gor. 10/1—7/3/25.**G.**
Gor. 23/7—17/9/27.**G.**
Gor. 13/4—18/5/29.**G.**
Gor. 14—21/9/29.**L.**
Gor. 5/3/32. *Not repaired.*

BOILERS:
127 28/11/14.
1897 24/7/20.
169 17/9/27.

SHEDS:
Northwich.
Sheffield 4/6/30.
Immingham 29/10/30.

RENUMBERED:
5709 7/3/25.

CONDEMNED: 5/3/32.
Cut up at Gorton.

_____

5710

Kitson & Co. 3450.

To traffic 12/1892.

REPAIRS:
Gor. ?/?—?/1/12.**G.**
Reb. with Standard No.1 boiler.
Gor. 23/10—27/11/15.**G.**
Gor. 11/5—27/7/18.**G.**
Gor. 19/11/21—28/1/22.**G.**
Gor. 8/12/23—29/3/24.**G.**
Gor. 20/2—17/4/26.**G.**
Gor. 19/5—7/7/28.**G.**

Gor. 9/1/30. *Not repaired.*

BOILERS:
119 27/11/15.
1750 27/7/18.
170 29/3/24.
53 17/4/26.
104 7/7/28.

SHED:
Barnsley.

RENUMBERED:
5710 17/5/24.

CONDEMNED: 9/1/30.
Cut up at Gorton.

_____

5711

Kitson & Co. 3451.

To traffic 12/1892.

REPAIRS:
Gor. ?/?—?/12/13.**G.**
*Rebuilt with Standard No.1
boiler.*
Gor. 30/6—1/9/17.**G.**
Gor. 21/8—19/2/21.**G.**
Gor. 24/11/23—26/1/24.**G.**

Gor. 15/8—14/11/25.**G.**
Gor. 3/9—22/10/27.**G.**
Gor. 18/1—8/2/30.**G.**
Gor. 26/6/33. *Not repaired.*

BOILERS:
394 1/9/17.
82 19/2/21.
1769 14/11/25.
306 8/2/30.

SHEDS:
New Holland.
Immingham 23/11/29.
New Holland 28/2/30.
Louth 14/7/30.
Immingham 28/4/33.

RENUMBERED:
5711 2/2/24.

CONDEMNED: 26/6/33.
Cut up at Gorton.

_____

Although the front buffers were all changed to parallel shank type, this did not apply to all the tenders. No.5687, at withdrawal on 22nd August 1935, still had original taper shank design. Gorton works.

No.684 became 5684 from 13th March 1926 and all its post-Grouping work was done in north and east Lincolnshire. From New Holland it moved to Louth on 14th July 1930 and here is at Cleethorpes about to return to Louth with this unusual load of nine coaches. It went to Immingham shed on 8th July 1932 and then back to New Holland on 28th December 1932.

Typical of its work from New Holland shed was this single coach working on the Barton-on-Humber branch, on which 5684 is arriving back at New Holland station. It had another spell from Immingham shed from 26th November 1934 to 13th September 1935. No.5684 finished its career at New Holland shed from 13th September 1935 to 16th June 1939 withdrawal.

Numbered 5710 from 29th March 1924, it did all its LNER work from Barnsley shed and here in late 1928 is arriving at Sheffield (Victoria) with newly rebuilt coaches from Doncaster. It was withdrawn 9th January 1930.

Despite maintenance by Gorton throughout their lives, most of the 1935 to 1937 withdrawals were sent to Doncaster for cutting up. Doncaster works.

Nos.508ʙ (condemned 11/7/23) and 511ʙ (condemned 8/11/23) remained in GCR livery. No.510ʙ had a general repair in November 1922 when this 'one-piece' chimney was put on and which it kept to withdrawal in March 1926. In clearing the GC Duplicate list, No.510ʙ became LNER 6415 when ex works 13th December 1924 from a further general repair. It was simply given one coat of black paint.

(below) Here at Nottingham (Victoria) prior to having the Duplicate B added in 1920, No.510 later worked at New Holland but by Grouping all three of the class were working on the CLC Southport line.

CLASS D 8

508B

Gorton.

To traffic 7/1888.

REPAIRS:
Gor. ?/?—?/5/12.**G.**
Reb. with Standard No.1 boiler.
Gor. 26/8—14/10/16.**G.**
Gor. 31/5—30/8/19.**G.**
Gor. 18/6—16/7/21.**G.**
Gor. 9/6/23. *Not repaired.*

BOILERS:
408 14/10/16.
1803 30/8/19.

SHEDS:
New Holland *by* 4/22.
Southport.

CONDEMNED: 11/7/23.
Cut up at Gorton.

_____

511B

Gorton.

To traffic 10/1888.

REPAIRS:
Gor. ?/?—?/12/10.**G.**
Reb. with Standard No.1 boiler.
Gor. 25/12/15—5/2/16.**G.**
Gor. 26/10/18—8/3/19.**G.**
Gor. 14/5—17/9/21.**G.**
Gor. 19/5—23/6/23.**G.**

BOILERS:
968 5/2/16.
735 8/3/19.
177 17/9/21.

SHEDS:
New Holland *at* 4/22.
Southport *by* 2/8/23.

CONDEMNED: 8/11/23.
Into Gor. for cut up 8/11/23.

_____

6415 (ex 510B)

Gorton.

To traffic 11/1888.

REPAIRS:
Gor. ?/?—?/5/10.**G.**
Reb. with Standard No.1 boiler.
Gor. 3/2—31/3/17.**G.**
Gor. 7/2—27/3/20.**G.**
Gor. 2/9—11/11/22.**G.**
Gor. 16/6—7/7/23.**G.**
Not painted.
Gor. 11/10—13/12/24.**G.**
Gor.6/3/26. *Not repaired.*

BOILERS:
942 31/3/17.
382 11/11/22.

SHEDS:
New Holland *by* 4/22.
Southport *by* 1925.

RENUMBERED:
6415 13/12/24.

CONDEMNED: 10/3/26.
Cut up at Gorton.

_____

(below) **No.6415 from 13th December 1924 was the LNER number given to 510**B **which did all its post-Grouping work from the sub shed at Southport where it is seen here. Its withdrawal on 10th March 1926 made D8 class extinct**

The second batch of the same order was for twenty, Nos.1018 to 1037, delivered February to May 1902.

(left) A further order for five, Nos.1038 to 1042, was delivered by Sharp Stewart & Co. during March 1903.

(below) The class was completed by an order for ten more engines, Nos.104 to 113, which Vulcan Foundry delivered from March to June 1904.

CLASS D 9

6013

Sharp Stewart 4784.

To traffic 10/1901.

REPAIRS:
Gor. 22/8—31/10/08.**G.**
Gor. 15/11/13—31/1/14.**G.**
Gor. 2/3—14/9/18.**G.**
Rebuilt with 5' 0" boiler.
Gor. 28/1—15/4/22.**G.**
Gor. 17/1—14/3/25.**G.**
Gor. 8/1—26/3/27.**G.**
Gor. 17/9—26/11/27.**G.**
Gor. 18/5—6/7/29.**G.**
Gor. 7/11—5/12/31.**G.**
Gor. 8—29/7/33.**G.**
Gor. 23/2—16/3/35.**G.**
To Part 2.
Gor. 13—27/2/37.**G.**
Tablet apparatus fitted.
To Part 1.
Don. 22/10—20/11/37.**L.**
Gor. 28/5—25/6/38.**G.**
To Part 2.
Gor. 9/3—6/4/40.**G.**
Gor. 12/12/42—9/1/43.**G.**
Gor. 25—28/8/43.**L.**
Gor. 8—29/6/46.**G.**
Gor. 7/2—20/3/48.**G.**
Gor. 26/3—9/4/49.**C/L.**

BOILERS:
94.
99 31/10/08.
1153 31/1/14.
1422 *(sup.)* 14/9/18.
281 14/3/25.
81 26/3/27.
411 5/12/31.
1780 29/7/33.
210 16/3/35.
719 27/2/37.
968 25/6/38.
3848 6/4/40.
796 9/1/43.
939 29/6/46.
3855 20/3/48.

SHEDS:
Lincoln 7/7/22.
Immingham *by* 1/1/35.
South Lynn 28/2/37.
Peterborough East 15/6/37.
South Lynn 12/8/37.
King's Lynn 8/11/39.
South Lynn 27/12/39.
Brunswick 4/8/46.
Trafford Park 14/12/47.

RENUMBERED:
6013 14/3/25.
2300 1/12/46.
62300 20/3/48.

CONDEMNED: 14/11/49.
Into Gor. for cut up 19/11/49 but cut up at Dukinfield..

6014

Sharp Stewart 4785.

To traffic 10/1901.

REPAIRS:
Gor. 26/6—7/8/09.**G.**
Gor. 27/2—20/3/15.**G.**
Gor. 17/5—20/12/19.**G.**
Rebuilt with 5' 0" boiler.
Intensifore fitted.
Gor. 10/12/21—25/3/22.**G.**
Gor. 28/6—4/10/24.**G.**
Gor. 21/8—27/11/26.**G.**
Gor. 3/9—5/11/27.**G.**
Gor. 10/8—21/9/29.**G.**
Gor. 21/3—25/4/31.**G.**
Gor. 11/3—1/4/33.**G.**
To Part 2.
Gor. 27/10—10/11/34.**G.**
Intensifore removed.
Gor. 29/8—26/9/36.**G.**
Gor. 16/7—27/8/38.**G.**
Gor. 4—18/11/39.**G.**
Gor. 8/5—6/6/42.**G.**
Gor. 1—23/10/43.**G.**
Gor. 2—9/3/46.**L.**
Gor. 12/10—16/11/46.**G.**
Gor. 16—23/8/47.**L.**
Gor. 12/6—3/7/48.**G.**
Gor. 30/10—27/11/48.**L.**
Gor. 29/4/50. *Not repaired.*

BOILERS:
77.
1339 7/8/09.
80 20/3/15.
1795 *(sup.)* 20/12/19.
396 21/9/29.
783 1/4/33.
149 10/11/34.
171 26/9/36.
774 18/11/39.
321 6/6/42.
653 23/10/43.
118 16/11/46.
174 3/7/48.

SHEDS:
Sheffield *at* 4/22.
Retford 28/11/27.
Sheffield 28/7/28.
Retford 6/10/28.
Sheffield 23/1/31.
Retford 14/5/31.
Sheffield 20/1/33.
Retford 4/5/33.
New England 16/5/41.
New Eng. M&GN 25/5/41.
Trafford Park 17/12/45.

RENUMBERED:
6014 4/10/24.
2301 16/11/46.
62301 3/7/48.

CONDEMNED: 29/4/50.
Cut up at Dar. 17/6/50.

6015

Sharp Stewart 4786.

To traffic 10/1901.

REPAIRS:
Gor. 16/11/12—28/6/13.**G.**
Rebuilt with 5' 0" boiler.
Gor. 25/2—6/5/22.**G.**
Gor. 29/3—12/7/24.**G.**
Gor. 13/11/26—22/1/27.**G.**
Gor. 13/4—18/5/29.**G.**
Gor. 14/3—25/4/31.**G.**
Gor. 27/5—24/6/33.**G.**
To Part 2.
Gor. 13/4—4/5/35.**G.**
To Part 1.
Gor. 17/7—7/8/37.**G.**
To Part 2.
Gor. 7—28/10/39.**G.**
Gor. 18/5—20/6/42.**G.**
Gor. 1—4/9/43.**L.**
Gor. 17/3—21/4/45.**G.**
Gor. 24/1—21/2/48.**G.**
Gor. 4/9/48.**L.**

BOILERS:
87.
1029A *(sup.)* 28/6/13.
1669 12/7/24.
276 25/4/31.
985 24/6/33.
718 4/5/35.
843 7/8/37.
936 28/10/39.
3855 20/6/42.
941 21/2/48.

SHEDS:
Sheffield 14/5/20.
Immingham 28/11/25.
Sheffield 18/12/25.
Retford 18/10/28.
Sheffield 23/11/28.
Retford 17/10/30.
Sheffield 5/1/31.
Retford 28/11/32.
Sheffield 27/3/33.
Retford 16/4/34.
Sheffield 18/8/34.
Lincoln 31/1/36.
March 4/5/36.
King's Lynn 10/5/36.
Peterborough East 18/2/37.
March 30/4/39.
South Lynn 22/6/43.
Brunswick 11/8/46.

RENUMBERED:
6015 12/7/24.
2302 24/11/46.
E2302 21/2/48.
62302 4/9/48.

CONDEMNED: 20/3/50.
Into Gorton for cut up 25/3/50.

6016

Sharp Stewart 4787.

To traffic 10/1901.

REPAIRS:
Gor. 9/3—8/6/12.**G.**
Gor. 10/6—25/11/16.**G.**
Rebuilt with 5' 0" boiler.
Gor. 9/4—11/6/21.**G.**
Gor. 25/8—27/10/23.**G.**
Gor. 25/4—25/7/25.**G.**
Gor. 2/4—4/6/27.**G.**
Gor. 20/4—15/6/29.**G.**
Gor. 23/1—13/2/32.**G.**
Gor. 20/1—3/2/34.**G.**
Gor. 25/1—15/2/36.**G.**
Gor. 28/5—18/6/38.**G.**
To Part 2.
Gor. 18/8—6/9/41.**G.**
Gor. 5—27/11/43.**G.**
Gor. 13/5—3/6/44.**L.**
Gor. 3/3/45.**L.**
Tender only.
Gor. 13/10/45.**L.**
Tender leaking badly.
Gor. 29/12/45—26/1/46.**G.**
Gor. 9/8—13/9/47.**G.**

In March 1907 No.104 was rebuilt with a 5ft 0in. instead of a 4ft 9in. boiler and the firebox was increased in length from 7ft 0in. to 8ft 6in. (shown by the extra washout plug). Cylinders became 19in. instead of 18½in. but still with slide valves. No.104 still had this boiler at Grouping and the name was put on at the 1907 rebuilding. Guide Bridge.

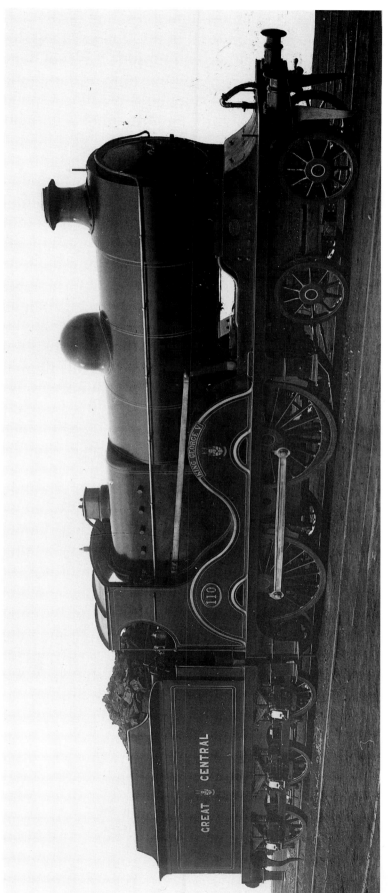

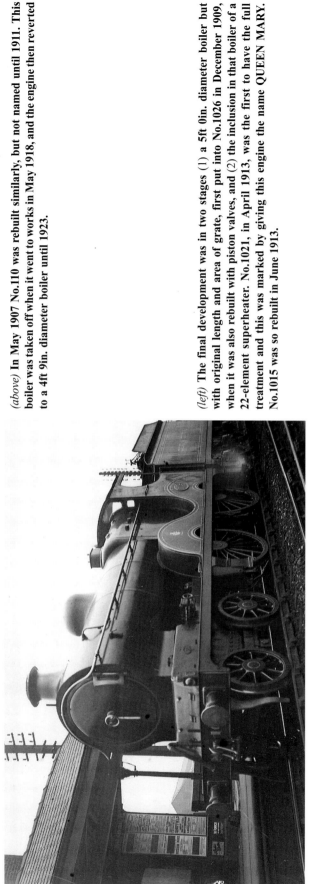

(above) In May 1907 No.110 was rebuilt similarly, but not named until 1911. This boiler was taken off when it went to works in May 1918, and the engine then reverted to a 4ft 9in. diameter boiler until 1923.

(left) The final development was in two stages (1) a 5ft 0in. diameter boiler but with original length and area of grate, first put into No.1026 in December 1909, when it was also rebuilt with piston valves, and (2) the inclusion in that boiler of a 22-element superheater. No.1021, in April 1913, was the first to have the full treatment and this was marked by giving this engine the name QUEEN MARY. No.1015 was so rebuilt in June 1913.

6016 cont./

BOILERS:
82.
885 8/6/12.
1644 *(sup.)* 25/11/16.
48 27/10/23.
416 15/6/29.
708 13/2/32.
384 3/2/34.
291 15/2/36.
708 18/6/38.
941 6/9/41.
942 27/11/43.
808 26/1/46.
119 13/9/47.

SHEDS:
Annesley 8/11/19.
Peterborough East 31/1/37.
New England 30/4/39.
Mexborough 27/2/40.
Doncaster 18/3/40.
Brunswick 9/5/42.
Heaton Mersey 7/6/42.
Trafford Park 8/6/43.
Brunswick 14/7/46.

RENUMBERED:
1016c 10/11/23.
6016 25/7/25.
2303 2/6/46.
62303 27/2/49 *at shed.*

CONDEMNED: 15/8/49.
Cut up at Dukinfield.

6017

Sharp Stewart 4788.

To traffic 10/1901.

REPAIRS:
Gor. 13/1—20/4/12.**G.**
Gor. 5/2—30/4/21.**G.**
Rebuilt with 5' 0" boiler.
Gor. 14/10—25/11/22.**G.**
Gor. 10/11/23—26/1/24.**G.**
Gor. 16/1—24/4/26.**G.**
Gor. 3/12/27—28/1/28.**G.**
Gor. 14/12/29—25/1/30.**G.**
Gor. 23/4—7/5/32.**G.**
Gor. 19/5—9/6/34.**G.**
To Part 2.
Gor. 8—29/2/36.**G.**
Gor. 23/10—20/11/37.**G.**
Gor. 8/7—5/8/39.**G.**
Gor. 29/4—23/5/42.**G.**
Gor. 12/3—3/4/43.**L.**
Gor. 4/12/43—15/1/44.**G.**
Gor. 24/11—22/12/45.**G.**
Gor. 25/10—6/12/47.**G.**

BOILERS:
80.
894 20/4/12.
1529 *(sup.)* 30/4/21.
1638 24/4/26.
278 7/5/32.
174 9/6/34.
118 29/2/36.
3844 20/11/37.
983 5/8/39.
985 15/1/44.
941 22/12/45.
774 6/12/47.

SHEDS:
Brunswick 14/10/21.
Sheffield 6/2/24.
Retford 23/11/28.
Sheffield 3/4/29.
Retford 20/1/33.
Sheffield 16/4/34.
Retford 23/6/34.
Sheffield 8/1/36.
Retford 10/3/36.
Sheffield 28/11/37.
Retford 29/1/38.
Brunswick 16/2/40.

RENUMBERED:
6017 26/1/24.
2304 21/7/46.
62304 27/2/49 *at shed.*

CONDEMNED: 16/1/50.
Into Gor. for cut up 21/1/50.

6018

Sharp Stewart 4828.

To traffic 2/1902.

REPAIRS:
Gor. 29/1—19/2/10.**G.**
Gor. 1/2—30/8/19.**G.**
Rebuilt with 5' 0" boiler.
Gor. 18/12/20—22/1/21.**G.**
Gor. 27/1—24/3/23.**G.**
Gor. 3/10/25—30/1/26.**G.**
Gor. 8/10—26/11/27.**G.**
Gor. 2/2—6/4/29.**G.**
Gor. 31/5—5/7/30.**G.**
Gor. 8—22/11/30.**L.**
Collision at Cleethorpes.
Gor. 21/5—2/7/32.**G.**
Gor. 30/9—14/10/33.**G.**
Gor. 16—30/11/35.**G.**
To Part 2.
Gor. 19/6—10/7/37.**G.**
Gor. 26/8—16/9/39.**G.**
Gor. 20/4—16/5/42.**G.**
Gor. 10/3—7/4/45.**G.**
Gor. 17/5—21/6/47.**G.**
Gor. 13/11—11/12/48.**G.**

BOILERS:
81.
889 19/2/10.
1784 *(sup.)* 30/8/19.
1694 30/1/26.
321 6/4/29.
386 14/10/33.
936 30/11/35.
774 10/7/37.
3850 16/9/39.
783 16/5/42.
119 7/4/45.
799 21/6/47.
816 11/12/48.

SHEDS:
Sheffield. 8/4/21.
Lincoln.
Immingham *by* 4/22.
Lincoln 28/12/32.
New Holland 18/5/35.
Lincoln 6/6/35.
King's Lynn 30/11/35.
Peterborough East 18/2/37.
March 30/4/39.
South Lynn 5/8/43.
March 8/10/43.
Stratford 18/12/45.
March 24/1/46.
South Lynn 30/5/46.
Northwich 11/8/46.
Trafford Park 10/8/47.

RENUMBERED:
6018 30/1/26.
2305 1/9/46.
62305 11/12/48.

CONDEMNED: 24/7/50.
Into Gor. for cut up 30/9/50 but sent to Darlington.

6019

Sharp Stewart 4829.

To traffic 2/1902.

REPAIRS:
Gor. 27/10/07—4/1/08.**G.**
Gor. 23/8—11/10/13.**G.**
Gor. 17/4—13/11/15.**G.**
Rebuilt with 5' 0" boiler.
Gor. 12/2—23/4/21.**G.**
Gor. 10/3—28/7/23.**G.**
Gor. 25/4—25/7/25.**G.**
Gor. 16/4—11/6/27.**G.**
Gor. 3/4—18/5/29.**G.**
Gor. 4/4—16/5/31.**G.**
Gor. 27/1—17/2/34.**G.**
To Part 2.
Gor. 2—30/5/36.**G.**
Gor. 23/10—13/11/37.**G.**
Gor. 17/6—1/7/39.**G.**

Gor. 21/11—20/12/41.**G.**
Gor. 3—29/1/44.**G.**
Gor. 17/8—7/9/46.**G.**
Gor. 28/6—5/7/47.**L.**
Frame fractured.

BOILERS:
83.
77 4/1/08.
91 11/10/13.
1562 *(sup.)* 13/11/15.
1583 25/7/25.
708 17/2/34.
810 30/5/36.
983 13/11/37.
3843 1/7/39.
696 20/12/41.
118 29/1/44.
3849 7/9/46.

SHEDS:
Gorton 27/7/19.
Sheffield 20/10/20.
Brunswick 12/8/35.
Peterborough East 26/1/38.
New England 30/4/39.
March 1/7/39.
South Lynn 23/4/43.
March 8/10/43.
Brunswick 10/3/46.

RENUMBERED:
1019c 1/9/23.
6019 25/7/25.
2306 21/7/46.

CONDEMNED: 12/1/49.
Cut up at Dukinfield.

6020

Sharp Stewart 4830.

To traffic 2/1902.

REPAIRS:
Gor. 11/10/13—28/3/14.**G.**
Rebuilt with 5' 0" boiler.
Gor. 20/5—5/8/22.**G.**
Gor. 4/10—20/12/24.**G.**
Gor. 24/10—7/11/25.**L.**
Gor. 25/9—18/12/26.**G.**
Gor. 16/6—14/7/28.**G.**
Gor. 14/12/29—18/1/30.**G.**
Gor. 12/3—2/4/32.**G.**
Gor. 10/6—1/7/33.**G.**
Gor. 8—22/6/35.**G.**
To Part 2.
Gor. 26/12/36—16/1/37.**G.**
Gor. 26/3—16/4/38.**G.**
Gor. 17/12/38—7/1/39.**L.**
Gor. 9/3—13/4/40.**G.**
Gor. 15—29/6/40.**L.**
Gor. 20/1/43. *Not repaired.*

In October 1918 the long firebox saturated boiler from No.110 was put on No.113, along with new piston valve cylinders and No.113 was in this hybrid condition until it went to works on 27th January 1923. Only seven, Nos.1042, 104, 105, 107, 110, 112 and 113 had not been superheated before Grouping, and No.6042 (in September 1924) was the only saturated engine to receive LNER livery. Manchester (London Road).

Superheater elements were initially protected from burning by a draught retarder or by Robinson's combined blower and circulating valve. By Grouping, all such devices had been removed, and some engines were still without this protection into the 1930's.

No example has been found of an anti-vacuum valve being put on whilst a D9 still had an original Robinson chimney. Nottingham (Victoria).

Even the first changes to 'plant pot' chimney were not coupled with the provision for superheater element protection. Nottingham (Victoria).

It was not until 24th March 1928 that a Gresley anti-vacuum valve was used on the D9 class when No.6022 was so fitted. In green livery, Nos.6028 and 6039 are the only others likely to be in same style as 6022. Nottingham (Victoria).

When No.5112 acquired boiler No.806 on 23rd March 1935, its superheater header had a Gresley anti-vacuum valve at each end. This boiler, new in October 1932, had been on No.6034 from May 1933 to February 1935 and after it came off No.5112 in February 1937, it served No.6042 from 27th March 1937 to 7th July 1939.

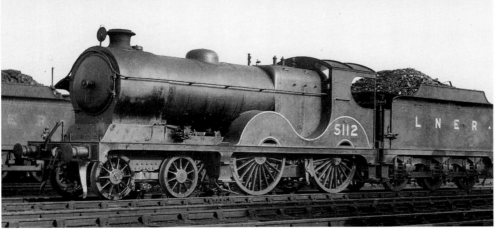

From 13th March 1937, No.5112 carried the normal single anti-vacuum valve in the standard place behind the chimney.

After the use of the Gresley type began in 1928, the whole class duly acquired this type, but only from 1931 in many instances.

6020 cont./

BOILERS:
84.
1341 *(sup.)* 28/3/14.
321 5/8/22.
325 14/7/28.
713 2/4/32.
596 1/7/33.
91 22/6/35.
119 16/1/37.
942 16/4/38.
968 13/4/40.

SHEDS:
Sheffield 14/5/20.
Brunswick 16/8/35.

RENUMBERED:
6020 20/12/24.

CONDEMNED: 3/2/43.
Cut up at Gorton.

6021

QUEEN MARY

Sharp Stewart 4831.

To traffic 2/1902.

REPAIRS:
Gor. 10/4—15/5/09.**G.**
Gor. 30/9—5/11/10.**G.**
Gor. 12/10/12—19/4/13.**G.**
Rebuilt with 5' 0" boiler.
Gor. 18/3—25/3/22.**G.**
Gor. 6/12/24—14/2/25.**G.**
Gor. 21/5—30/7/27.**G.**
Gor. 23/2—6/4/29.**G.**
Gor. 28/2—28/3/31.**G.**
Gor. 15/4—13/5/33.**G.**
To Part 2.
Gor. 13/7—10/8/35.**G.**
Gor. 3/4—1/5/37.**G.**
Tablet apparatus fitted.
To Part 1.
Gor. 9—30/7/38.**G.**
To Part 2.
Gor. 16/3—6/4/40.**G.**
Gor. 27/7—14/8/43.**G.**
Gor. 12/10—2/11/46.**G.**
Gor. 13/9/47.**L.**
Tender only.
Gor. 4—25/9/48.**G.**
Gor. 4/12/48.**L.**
Tender only.

BOILERS:
85.
886 15/5/09.
890 5/11/10.
1194 *(sup.)* 19/4/13.
1583 25/3/22.

1029A 14/2/25.
413 28/3/31.
653 13/5/33.
846 10/8/35.
416 1/5/37.
149 30/7/38.
810 6/4/40.
714 14/8/43.
3867 2/11/46.
3859 2/11/46.

SHEDS:
Lincoln 1/9/22.
Immingham 15/8/24.
Lincoln 21/8/24.
Immingham.
Leicester 21/7/33.
Mexborough 29/9/33.
South Lynn 7/6/37.
March 2/10/37.
South Lynn 16/11/37.
Melton Constable 21/1/38.
March 20/9/39.
King's Lynn 21/8/44.
March 27/5/45.
Trafford Park 11/3/46.
Heaton Mersey 11/9/49.

RENUMBERED:
6021 14/2/25.
2307 21/7/46.
62307 25/9/48.

CONDEMNED: 12/6/50.
Into Gor. for cut up 17/6/50.

6022

Sharp Stewart 4832.

To traffic 2/1902.

REPAIRS:
Gor. ?/?—22/6/07.**G.**
Gor. 23/8—4/10/13.**G.**
Gor. 20/1—2/6/17.**G.**
Rebuilt with 5' 0" boiler.
Gor. 27/5—2/9/22.**G.**
Gor. 9/8—25/10/24.**G.**
Gor. 6/3—29/5/26.**G.**
Gor. 8/1—26/4/27.**G.**
Gor. 11/2—24/3/28.**G.**
Gor. 21/11/29—8/2/30.**G.**
Gor. 14/11—19/12/31.**G.**
Gor. 6/1—3/2/34.**G.**
To Part 2.
Gor. 3—10/3/34.**L.**
After collision.
Gor. 2—23/5/36.**G.**
Gor. 2—30/4/38.**G.**
Gor. 4—25/5/40.**G.**
Gor. 6/8/42. *Not repaired.*

BOILERS:
87.
86.
451 *(new)* 22/6/07.
321 4/10/13.
1669 *(sup.)* 2/6/17.
325 2/9/22.
453 24/3/28.
810 3/2/34.
714 23/5/36.
119 30/4/38.
672 25/5/40.

SHEDS:
Annesley 8/12/22.
Colwick 2/4/28.
Peterborough East 22/7/34.
New England 28/7/34.
Ipswich 9/8/34.
Sheffield 12/3/35.
Retford 4/7/36.
Brunswick 19/2/40.

RENUMBERED:
6022 25/10/24.

CONDEMNED: 22/8/42.
Cut up at Gorton.

6023

Sharp Stewart 4833.

To traffic 2/1902.

REPAIRS:
Gor. 9/11/12—3/5/13.**G.**
Rebuilt with 5' 0" boiler.
Gor. 21/8—6/11/20.**G.**
Gor. 31/3—25/8/23.**G.**
Gor. 30/5—28/11/25.**G.**
Gor. 20/8—15/10/27.**G.**
Gor. 13/4—18/5/29.**G.**
Gor. 2/5—6/6/31.**G.**
Gor. 1—29/4/33.**G.**
Gor. 6—20/7/35.**G.**
To Part 2.
Gor. 31/10—21/11/36.**G.**
Gor. 18/6—9/7/38.**G.**
Gor. 4/2—11/3/39.**G.**
Gor. 19/4—17/5/41.**G.**
Gor. 26/10—13/11/43.**G.**
Gor. 2/3—6/4/46.**G.**
Gor. 11—25/5/46.**L.**
Gor. 29/5—12/6/48.**G.**
Gor. 12/2—12/6/49.**L.**
Boiler backplate fracture.

BOILERS:
89.
86 *(sup.)* 3/5/13.
1780 28/11/25.
653 6/6/31.
444 29/4/33.

672 20/7/35.
149 21/11/36.
714 9/7/38.
985 17/5/41.
939 13/11/43.
942 6/4/46.
985 12/6/48.

SHEDS:
Annesley 4/3/21.
Trafford Park 2/11/35.
Brunswick 10/2/38.

RENUMBERED:
1023c 22/9/23.
6023 28/11/25.
2308 21/7/46.
62308 12/6/48.

CONDEMNED: 15/8/49.
Cut up at Dukinfield.

6024

Sharp Stewart 4834.

To traffic 2/1902.

REPAIRS:
Gor. 11/1—28/3/08.**G.**
Gor. 31/10/14—17/4/15.**G.**
Rebuilt with 5' 0" boiler.
Gor. 14/5—2/7/21.**G.**
Gor. 27/10/23—9/2/24.**G.**
Gor. 17/10/25—6/2/26.**G.**
Gor. 26/3—21/5/27.**G.**
Gor. 1/12/28—26/1/29.**G.**
Gor. 22/2—29/3/30.**G.**
Gor. 21/11—12/12/31.**G.**
Gor. 28/1—11/2/33.**G.**
Gor. 10/3—14/4/34.**G.**
To Part 2.
Gor. 18/5—8/6/35.**G.**
To Part 1.
Gor. 4—31/12/37.**G.**
To Part 2.
Gor. 31/12/38—28/1/39.**G.**
Gor. 10/2—9/3/40.**G.**
Gor. 1/9—1/11/41.**G.**
Gor. 17/1—19/2/44.**G.**
Gor. 10/11—8/12/45.**G.**
Gor. 23/8—13/9/47.**G.**

BOILERS:
90.
97 28/3/08.
941 *(sup.)* 17/4/15.
1426 2/7/21.
86 6/2/26.
384 26/1/29.
696 12/12/31.
168 11/2/33.
91 14/4/34.
720 8/6/35.

6024 cont./
118 31/12/37.
3848 28/1/39.
3851 9/3/40.
941 19/2/44.
3842 8/12/45.
772 13/9/47.

SHEDS:
Lincoln 19/5/22.
Immingham.
New Holland 20/2/29.
Immingham 11/1/30.
New Holland 24/4/30.
Immingham 22/9/31.
New Holland 31/12/31.
Immingham 26/10/32.
New Holland 11/3/33.
Immingham 12/2/34.
New Holland 3/5/34.
March 6/6/35.
King's Lynn 4/7/35.
Peterborough East 26/11/35.
Brunswick 26/1/38.

RENUMBERED:
6024 9/2/24.
2309 21/7/46.
62309 27/2/49 *at shed.*

CONDEMNED: 21/11/49.
Into Gor. for cut up 26/11/49 but cut up at Dukinfield.

6025

Sharp Stewart 4835.

To traffic 3/1902.

REPAIRS:
Gor. 24/11/09—8/1/10.**G.**
Gor. 18/4—1/8/14.**G.**
Rebuilt with 5' 0" boiler.
Gor. 25/12/20—5/2/21.**G.**
Gor. 27/1—5/5/23.**G.**
Gor. 31/1—28/3/25.**G.**
Gor. 4/9—4/12/26.**G.**
Gor. 30/6—11/8/28.**G.**
To Part 2.
Gor. 28/6—2/8/30.**G.**
Gor. 6/8—17/9/32.**G.**
T Part 1.
Gor. 21/7—4/8/34.**G.**
To Part 2.
Gor. 8—22/2/36.**G.**
To Part 1.
Gor. 23/7—13/8/38.**G.**
To Part 2.
Gor. 12/12/41—10/1/42.**G.**

Gor. 17/1—12/2/44.**G.**
Gor. 31/3/45.**L.**
Tender only.
Gor. 20/10/45. *Not repaired.*

BOILERS:
263 8/1/10.
414 *(sup.)* 1/8/14.
1686 5/5/23.
844 11/8/28.
391 17/9/32.
772 4/8/34.
384 22/2/36.
783 13/8/38.
957 10/1/42.
808 12/2/44.

SHEDS:
Annesley 14/5/20.
Colwick 2/4/28.
Annesley 5/5/33.
Colwick 12/10/33.
Peterborough East 23/6/36.
New England 30/4/39.
Mexborough 28/2/40.
Doncaster 18/3/40.
Heaton Mersey 1/6/42.

RENUMBERED:
6025 28/3/25.
2310 allocated.

CONDEMNED: 6/11/45.
Cut up at Gorton.

6026

Sharp Stewart 4836.

To traffic 3/1902.

REPAIRS:
Gor. 10/8—9/11/07.**G.**
Gor. 16/11—25/12/09.**G.**
Rebuilt with 5' 0" sat. boiler.
Gor. 13/6—3/10/14.**G.**
Rebuilt with 5' 0" sup. boiler.
Gor. 18/11—16/12/22.**G.**
Gor. 22/11/24—24/1/25.**G.**
Gor. 25/12/26—5/3/27.**G.**
Gor. 3/11/28—5/1/29.**G.**
Gor. 6/12/30—10/1/31.**G.**
Gor. 6—27/5/33.**G.**
To Part 2.
Gor. 29/6—13/7/35.**G.**
To Part 1.
Gor. 2—30/10/37.**G.**
To Part 2.
Gor. 11/11—2/12/39.**G.**
Gor. 26/3—17/4/43.**G.**

Gor. 18/11—2/12/44.**L.**
Gor. 11/1—1/2/47.**G.**

BOILERS:
91.
90 9/11/07.
677 25/12/09.
453 *(sup.)* 3/10/14.
121 16/12/22.
985 10/1/31.
846 27/5/33.
596 13/7/35.
957 30/10/37.
171 2/12/39.
3848 17/4/43.
3843 1/2/47.

SHEDS:
Sheffield 29/10/20.
Retford 6/7/36.
New England 16/5/41.
New Eng. M&GN 2/6/41.
Brunswick 18/12/45.
Walton-on-the-Hill 13/4/47.

RENUMBERED:
6026 24/1/25.
2311 2/6/46.
62311 12/3/49.

CONDEMNED: 18/7/49.
Into Gor. for cut up 23/7/49 but cut up at Dukinfield.

6027

Sharp Stewart 4837.

To traffic 3/1902.

REPAIRS:
Gor. 8/10—28/11/08.**G.**
Gor. 17/6—15/7/11.**G.**
Gor. 26/6—31/7/20.**G.**
Rebuilt with 5' 0" boiler.
Gor. 25/11/22—20/1/23.**G.**
Gor. 15/11/24—7/2/25.**G.**
Gor. 15/1—19/3/27.**G.**
Gor. 10/11—22/12/28.**G.**
Gor. 19/7—6/9/30.**G.**
Gor. 5/3—2/4/32.**G.**
Gor. 9—30/12/33.**G.**
Mech. lub. to cylinders.
Gor. 20/7—17/8/35.**G.**
To Part 2.
Gor. 23/1—6/2/37.**G.**
Gor. 12/11—24/12/38.**G.**
Gor. 19/10—9/11/40.**G.**
Gor. 15/10—7/11/42.**G.**
Gor. 10—28/10/44.**G.**

Gor. 7/12/46—4/1/47.**G.**
Gor. 18/9—9/10/48.**G.**

BOILERS:
92.
891 28/11/08.
319 15/7/11.
1905 *(sup.)* 31/7/20.
1684 19/3/27.
416 2/4/32.
366 30/12/33.
653 17/8/35.
91 6/2/37.
845 24/12/38.
119 9/11/40.
774 7/11/42.
3843 28/10/44.
708 4/1/47.
3867 9/10/48.

SHEDS:
Sheffield 3/11/20.
Immingham 29/12/28.
New England 22/9/31.
Immingham 31/12/31.
New Holland 12/2/34.
Immingham 3/9/34.
New Holland 24/7/34.
Immingham 6/6/35.
Peterborough East 29/6/36.
King's Lynn 14/5/38.
Immingham 12/5/39.
Brunswick 3/8/43.
Trafford Park 14/12/47.

RENUMBERED:
1027c ?/?/?
6027 7/2/25.
2312 2/6/46.
62312 9/10/48.

CONDEMNED: 24/4/50.
Into Gor. for cut up 29/4/50 but sent to Dar. and cut up 17/6/50.

6028

Sharp Stewart 4838.

To traffic 3/1902.

REPAIRS:
Gor. 3/5—7/6/13.**G.**
Gor. 10/10—19/12/14.**G.**
Rebuilt with 5' 0" boiler.
Gor. 19/2—7/5/21.**G.**
Gor. 6/1—17/2/23.**G.**
Gor. 26/7—11/10/24.**G.**
Gor. 12/12/25—29/5/26.**G.**
Gor. 8/1—2/4/27.**G.**

WORKS CODES:- Bpk - Beyer, Peacock. Cow - Cowlairs. Dar- Darlington. Don - Doncaster. Efd - Eastfield. Ghd - Gateshead. Gor - Gorton. Inv - Inverurie. Str - Stratford. Wfd - Woodford.
REPAIR CODES:- **C/H** - Casual Heavy. **C/L** - Casual Light. **G** - General. **H** - Heavy. **H/I** - Heavy Intermediate. **L** - Light. **L/I** - Light Intermediate. **N/C** - Non-Classified.

54

Superheated engines were normally provided with a Wakefield mechanical lubricator for the cylinders and valves but two exceptions were recorded.

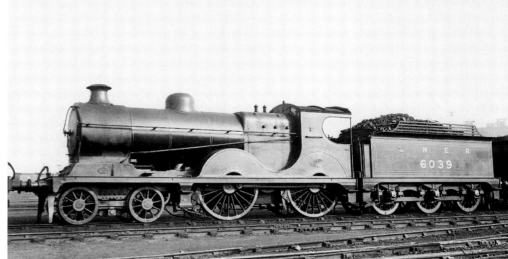

From July 1926 (at least) No.6039 had a sight feed lubricator in the cab with two inclined pipes to the cylinders and valves. It is not known when this was changed to Wakefield mechanical.

Until October 1934 No.6014 had a Robinson Intensifore type sight feed lubricator for the cylinders and valves. When ex works on 10th November 1934 this had been replaced by a Wakefield type. Sheffield Neepsend shed.

In early LNER years, firebox washout facilities on the left-hand side, were by two hand holes on the shoulder and three large plugs on the side.

On the right hand side, there were also two hand holes on the shoulder, but four large plugs on the side, staggered with those opposite.

From about 1930, replacement boilers had the same washout arrangement but the plugs were smaller. Sheffield Neepsend shed.

The change to smaller plugs was also made to the four on the right hand side. Note that it was effected whilst the boilers still had a dome to the original height.

The original dome had a height of 13ft 1in. from rail level but this was cut to only 12ft 3in. on new boilers built from March 1928. The 'plant pot' type chimney, combined with moving the whistle from the cab top to the firebox top, brought all heights within the 13ft 0in. composite loading gauge. No.6025, in August 1928, and No.6031 in September 1928, were the first under 13ft 0in. but no more were done until April 1933 and No.6036, in December 1938, was the last to complete this alteration. Many of the class reverted to being over 13ft. high during this period when older boilers were refitted. No.6025 actually reverted twice. No.6037's date was April 1935.

During the 1939-45 war, one or two acquired a new dome cover of a more angular shape.

On D9 class the original Robinson chimney proved to be longer lived than on most other classes. Some were not replaced until early 1932, and their large base diameter precluded the use with them of the Gresley anti-vacuum valve. Sheffield Neepsend shed.

The first replacements were made in 1925 by a 'plant pot', type 1ft 9in. high, which left the height from rail level still at 13ft 3in. No.5111 got this type in December 1925. Gorton shed.

From 1928, when the first move was made to bring this class under 13ft 0in., a 1ft 5½in. 'plant pot' chimney was used but the taller variety was in use to 1933.

In 1933 when a determined effort began to bring the D9 class within the 13ft 0in. load gauge, a new chimney design was introduced. Superseding the 'plant pot' type it was akin to the Robinson original, but shorter and with a smaller diameter base, so that there was no interference with the anti-vacuum valve. By 1938 the whole class had received it.

Well before Grouping, the whole class had parallel shank buffers and this type was continued to withdrawal in most cases, only three late exceptions being noted.

Between April and November 1946, Nos.2306, 2313 and 2317 had their GCR design buffers replaced by the Group Standard type.

6028 cont./

Gor. 7/4—26/5/28.**G.**
Gor. 24/8—12/10/29.**G.**
Gor. 14/11—19/12/31.**G.**
Gor. 17/6—8/7/33.**G.**
To Part 2.
Gor. 17—31/8/35.**G.**
To Part 1.
Gor. 29/5—12/6/37.**G.**
To Part 2.
Gor. 5/5/39. *Not repaired.*

BOILERS:
93.
80 7/6/13.
596 *(sup.)* 19/12/14.
253 7/5/21.
1426 29/5/26.
1784 19/12/31.
713 8/7/33.
366 31/8/35.
3843 12/6/37.

SHEDS:
Annesley *at* 4/22.
Colwick 2/4/28.
Annesley 29/10/28.
Colwick 21/6/37.
Lincoln 19/7/37.
King's Lynn 3/6/38.

RENUMBERED:
6028 11/10/24.

CONDEMNED: 5/5/39.
Cut up at Gorton.

6029

Sharp Stewart 4839.

To traffic 3/1902.

REPAIRS:
Gor. 20/4—18/6/10.**G.**
Gor. 11/11/11—17/2/12.**G.**
Gor. 8/3—25/10/13.**G.**
Rebuilt with 5' 0" boiler.
Gor. 27/5—5/8/22.**G.**
Gor. 9/8—1/11/24.**G.**
Gor. 21/8—20/11/26.**G.**
Gor. 22/9—17/11/28.**G.**
Gor. 24/5—28/6/30.**G.**
Gor. 31/12/31—6/2/32.**G.**
Gor. 7—28/10/33.**G.**
Gor. 28/12/35—18/1/36.**G.**
Gor. 22/1—12/2/38.**G.**
To Part 2.
Gor. 10—24/6/39.**G.**
Gor. 27/4—4/5/40.**L.**
Gor. 11/8—22/11/41.**G.**
Gor. 20—25/7/42.**L.**
Gor. 30/9—23/10/43.**G.**
Gor. 3—7/10/44.**L.** *Tender only.*

Gor. 23/12/44—3/2/45.**G.**
Gor. 19/10—23/11/46.**G.**
Gor. 6—20/9/47.**L.**
Gor. 27/3/48.**L.** *Tender only.*
Gor. 26/6—21/8/48.**G.**

BOILERS:
95.
86 18/6/10.
321 17/2/12.
281 *(sup.)* 25/10/13.
558 1/11/24.
1644 28/6/30.
704 6/2/32.
291 28/10/33.
1669 18/1/36.
808 12/2/38.
816 24/6/39.
942 *(ex6030)* 22/11/41.
719 23/10/43.
936 3/2/45.
3844 23/11/46.
118 21/8/48.

SHEDS:
Sheffield 31/7/20.
Immingham 19/12/28.
New Holland 26/10/32.
Immingham 11/3/33.
Louth 7/12/38.
Trafford Park 2/4/42.

RENUMBERED:
6029 1/11/24.
2313 21/7/46.
62313 27/3/48.

CONDEMNED: 10/10/49.
Cut up at Dukinfield.

6030

Sharp Stewart 4840.

To traffic 3/1902.

REPAIRS:
Gor. 21/10—20/11/09.**G.**
Gor. 28/4—20/5/11.**G.**
Gor. 29/5—20/11/15.**G.**
Rebuilt with 5' 0" boiler.
Gor. 29/4—15/7/22.**G.**
Ross 'pops' fitted.
Gor. 13/9—15/11/24.**G.**
Gor. 9/4—4/6/27.**G.**
Gor. 13/4—25/5/29.**G.**
Gor. 16/5—20/6/31.**G.**
Gor. 25/3—8/4/33.**G.**
To Part 2.
Gor. 2—16/2/35.**G.**
Gor. 31/12/36—16/1/37.**G.**
Gor. 11/6—9/7/38.**G.**
Gor. 30/3—13/4/40.**G.**
Gor. 14/10—1/11/41.**G.**

Gor. 11—25/11/44.**G.**
Gor. 6/9—4/10/47.**G.**

BOILERS:
96.
91 20/11/09.
886 20/5/11.
1572 *(sup.)* 20/11/15.
291 15/7/22.
444 20/6/31.
796 8/4/33.
658 16/2/35.
672 16/1/37.
942 13/4/40.
708 1/11/41.
774 25/11/44.
3842 4/10/47.

SHEDS:
Sheffield 29/12/22.
Retford 29/9/30.
Sheffield 8/7/31.
Lincoln 12/10/31.
New Holland 6/6/35.
Immingham 31/3/39.
Retford 24/3/41.
New England 20/5/41.
New Eng. M&GN 2/6/41.
Heaton Mersey 19/12/45.

RENUMBERED:
6030 15/11/24.
2314 28/7/46.
62314 12/2/49.

CONDEMNED: 9/5/49.
Into Gor. for cut up 14/5/49 but cut up at Dukinfield.

6031

Sharp Stewart 4841.

To traffic 3/1902.

REPAIRS:
Gor. 8/6—14/9/07.**G.**
Gor. 16/11—14/12/12.**G.**
Gor. 15/1—12/2/16.**G.**
Gor. 7/1—22/4/22.**G.**
Rebuilt with 5' 0" boiler.
Gor. 21/6—16/8/24.**G.**
Gor. 25/9—11/12/26.**G.**
Gor. 21/7—15/9/28.**G.**
To Part 2.
Gor. 1/2—15/5/30.**G.**
Gor. 16/4—4/6/32.**G.**
Gor. 12/1—2/2/35.**G.**
Gor. 5—26/6/37.**G.**
Gor. 3—24/12/38.**G.**
Gor. 26/8/39.**L.**
Gor. 29/3—5/4/41.**L.**
Tender damaged by enemy action at Cambridge.

Gor. 30/4—16/5/42.**G.**
Gor. 26/9—3/10/42.**L.**
Gor. 3—17/11/45.**G.**
Gor. 9—23/2/46.**L.**
Gor. 20/3—26/6/48.**G.**

BOILERS:
97.
79 14/9/07.
890 14/12/12.
887 12/2/16.
276 *(sup.)* 22/4/22.
845 15/9/28.
774 2/2/35.
772 26/6/37.
321 24/12/38.
3841 16/5/42.
3846 17/11/45.
942 26/6/48.

SHEDS:
Sheffield 2/10/17.
Staveley 26/9/32.
Sheffield 27/3/33.
Norwich 9/3/35.
Peterborough East 25/11/35.
King's Lynn 30/4/39.
Cambridge 19/6/39.
March 31/5/42.
Brunswick 26/7/46.

RENUMBERED:
6031 16/8/24.
2315 1/9/46.
62315 26/6/48.

CONDEMNED: 18/7/49.
Into Gor. for cut up 23/7/49 but cut up at Dukinfield.

6032

Sharp Stewart 4842.

To traffic 3/1902.

REPAIRS:
Gor. 13/10—4/12/09.**G.**
Gor. 14/10—4/11/11.**G.**
Gor. 23/4—11/6/21.**G.**
Rebuilt with 5' 0" boiler.
Gor. 3/11/23—26/1/24.**G.**
Gor. 11—25/10/24.**L.**
Gor. 12/12/25—27/3/26.**G.**
Gor. 24/9—12/11/27.**G.**
Gor. 15/6—10/8/29.**G.**
Gor. 27/6—25/7/31.**G.**
Gor. 17/6—8/7/33.**G.**
Gor. 28/9—12/10/35.**G.**
Gor. 29/5—26/6/37.**G.**
Gor. 24/12/38—21/1/39.**G.**
To Part 2.
Gor. 24/5—21/6/41.**G.**
Gor. 17/1—5/2/44.**G.**

The standard safety valve equipment was four Ramsbottom type enclosed in a rectangular brass casing, but by Grouping, changes had already begun. Nottingham (Victoria).

From the early 1920's the brass casing was gradually discarded and by 1926 had virtually disappeared, the last to carry one - to April 1928 - was probably No.5111.

The open Ramsbottom valves survived at least until No.5108 went for repair in March 1932 although by Grouping, Ross 'pop' valves had become the standard.

When No.1014 was rebuilt and superheated in December 1919 its newly built boiler had two Ross 'pop' safety valves, and from then on, they gradually became the standard.

Ex works on 3rd March 1923, No.1037 had changed to a boiler built in 1914. The Ramsbottom valves had been discarded and the mounting had been adapted to take two Ross 'pop' valves. Manchester (Central).

(below) From 1919 new boilers had the 'pop' valves mounted directly on to the firebox and all gradually took this form.

6032 cont./
Gor. 3/3/45. *Not repaired.*

BOILERS:
   98.
   96 4/12/09.
   892 4/11/11.
   596 *(sup.)* 11/6/21.
1529 27/3/26.
1905 10/8/29.
1780 25/7/31.
   276 8/7/33.
1905 12/10/35.
1597 26/6/37.
   91 21/1/39.
   816 21/6/41.
   983 5/2/44.

SHEDS:
Sheffield 2/12/21.
Annesley 7/4/26.
Staveley 12/5/39.
Langwith Jct. 4/11/41.
Staveley 23/12/41.
Brunswick 4/3/43.

RENUMBERED:
6032 26/1/24.
2316 allocated.

CONDEMNED: 3/3/45.
Cut up at Gorton.

6033

Sharp Stewart 4843.

To traffic 3/1902.

REPAIRS:
Gor. 2/5—20/6/08.**G.**
Gor. 12/6/15—15/1/16.**G.**
Rebuilt with 5' 0" boiler.
Gor. 11/3—22/4/22.**G.**
Gor. 29/3—21/6/24.**G.**
Gor. 23/1—27/3/26.**G.**
Gor. 21/5—16/7/27.**G.**
Gor. 19/1—23/2/29.**G.**
Gor. 14/2—21/3/31.**G.**
Gor. 22/8—10/10/31.**L.**
Gor. 29/4—13/5/33.**G.**
Gor. 11/5—1/6/35.**G.**
Gor. 10—31/10/36.**G.**
To Part 2.
Gor. 2—23/4/38.**G.**
Gor. 30/12/39—27/1/40.**G.**
Gor. 19/11/41—3/1/42.**G.**
Gor. 19—27/3/43.**L.**
Gor. 23—28/8/43.**L.**
Gor. 6—25/3/44.**G.**
Gor. 9/3—13/4/46.**G.**
Gor. 7/8—11/9/48.**G.**

BOILERS:
   99.
   323 20/6/08.
1583 *(sup.)* 15/1/16.
   278 22/4/22.
1905 16/7/27.
   846 23/2/29.
   720 13/5/33.
   411 1/6/35.
   968 31/10/36.
3846 23/4/38.
   957 27/1/40.
3843 3/1/42.
3847 25/3/44.
   816 13/4/46.
   964 11/9/48.

SHEDS:
Annesley *at* 4/22.
Trafford Park 29/10/35.

RENUMBERED:
6033 21/6/24.
2317 19/7/46.
62317 11/9/48.

CONDEMNED: 18/7/49.
Into Gor. for cut up 23/7/49 but cut up at Dukinfield.

6034

Sharp Stewart 4844.

To traffic 3/1902.

REPAIRS:
Gor. 21/2—1/8/14.**G.**
Rebuilt with 5' 0" boiler.
Gor. 21/8/20—26/2/21.**G.**
Gor. 3/2—7/4/23.**G.**
Gor. 16/2—29/3/24.**L.**
Gor. 11/4—18/7/25.**G.**
Gor. 3/9—29/10/27.**G.**
Gor. 5/10—9/11/29.**G.**
Gor. 11/4—23/5/31.**G.**
Gor. 29/4—13/5/33.**G.**
To Part 2.
Gor. 23/2—9/3/35.**G.**
To Part 1.
Gor. 30/1—13/2/37.**G.**
To Part 2.
Gor. 31/12/38—28/1/39.**G.**
Gor. 18/1—15/2/41.**G.**
Gor. 7—14/8/43.**G.**
Gor. 3—24/3/45.**G.**
Gor. 11/10—15/11/47.**G.**

BOILERS:
   100.
   253 *(sup.)* 1/8/14.
1531 26/2/21.
   410 9/11/29.
   806 13/5/33.

719 9/3/35.
658 13/2/37.
985 28/1/39.
844 15/2/41.
171 14/8/43.
704 24/3/45.
808 15/11/47.

SHEDS:
Sheffield 19/5/22.
Lincoln 21/10/31.
Leicester 21/7/33.
Mexborough 29/9/33.
Brunswick 15/8/43.

RENUMBERED:
6034 29/3/24.
2318 28/7/46.
62318 5/2/49.

CONDEMNED: 21/11/49.
Into Gor. for cut up 26/11/49 but cut up at Dukinfield.

6035

Sharp Stewart 4845.

To traffic 4/1902.

REPAIRS:
Gor. ?/?—1/6/07.**G.**
Gor. 31/1—18/4/14.**G.**
Rebuilt with 5' 0" boiler.
Gor. 8/5—10/7/20.**G.**
Gor. 3/2—21/7/23.**G.**
Gor. 14/3—6/6/25.**G.**
Gor. 20/11/26—29/1/27.**G.**
Gor. 26/1—16/3/29.**G.**
Gor. 21/2—28/3/31.**G.**
Gor. 11/3—29/4/33.**G.**
Gor. 8/12/34—5/1/35.**G.**
To Part 2.
Gor. 16—30/5/36.**G.**
Gor. 2—30/4/38.**G.**
Gor. 4/5—1/6/40.**G.**
Gor. 11—15/8/42.**L.**
Gor. 21/4—8/5/43.**G.**
Gor. 3—8/4/44.**L.**
Gor. 27/1—3/2/45.**L.**
Gor. 25/1—15/2/47.**G.**

BOILERS:
   92 1/6/07.
   48 *(sup.)* 18/4/14.
1572 21/7/23.
1686 16/3/29.
   783 5/1/35.
   708 30/5/36.
   704 30/4/38.
   719 1/6/40.
3845 8/5/43.
   986 15/2/47.

SHEDS:
Annesley *at* 4/22.
Colwick 2/4/28.
King's Lynn 30/5/36.
Cambridge 16/6/39.
Lincoln 21/9/39.
Doncaster 16/2/40.
New England 24/9/42.
Brunswick 20/12/45.

RENUMBERED:
1035c 1/9/23.
6035 6/6/25.
2319 28/7/46.
62319 19/3/49.

CONDEMNED: 18/7/49.
Into Gor. for cut up 18/7/49 but cut up at Dukinfield.

6036

Sharp Stewart 4846.

To traffic 4/1902.

REPAIRS:
Gor. 7/7—1/8/08.**G.**
Gor. 20/10/11—20/1/12.**G.**
Gor. 14/8—13/11/15.**G.**
Gor. 26/10/18—10/5/19.**G.**
Rebuilt with 5' 0" boiler.
Gor. 9/4—28/5/21.**G.**
Gor. 4/8—13/10/23.**G.**
Gor. 28/3—4/7/25.**G.**
Gor. 5/3—30/4/27.**G.**
Gor. 24/11/28—12/1/29.**G.**
Gor. 24/1—28/2/31.**G.**
Gor. 25/2—11/3/33.**G.**
Gor. 29/9—20/10/34.**G.**
Gor. 31/12/36—23/1/37.**G.**
Gor. 3—31/12/38.**G.**
To Part 2.
Gor. 1—29/6/40.**G.**
Gor. 21/5—27/6/42.**G.**
Gor. 19/3—3/4/43.**G.**
Gor. 12/8—2/9/44.**G.**
Gor. 12—19/5/45.**L.**

BOILERS:
   78 1/8/08.
   85 20/1/12.
   184 13/11/15.
1780 *(sup.)* 10/5/19.
1428 4/7/25.
   276 12/1/29.
   720 28/2/31.
   696 11/3/33.
   391 20/10/34.
   276 23/1/37.
   395 31/12/38.
   704 29/6/40.
   986 27/6/42.
   149 2/9/44.

The GCR had begun fitting ash ejectors just prior to Grouping and the steam supply to them entered the rear of the smokebox. Nottingham (Victoria).

By 1925 it had been found that this steam entry point caused scouring of the front tube plate, so the pipe was lengthened to provide an entry point into the front part of the smokebox. All were either fitted or altered to this arrangement. Sheffield Neepsend shed.

(below) During 1946, removal of the ash ejector began, and only No.2325 of the renumbered engines was noted as still so fitted. This was probably due to its previous general repair being in October 1945.

Until 1945 the top lamp iron was fixed above the smokebox and the fastening of the door was by a wheel and a handle.

Soon after the war, the lamp iron was lowered and fixed on the smokebox door. The wheel for fastening the door was also replaced by another handle.

In the period 1934 to 1939, many of the D9 class worked from ex-GER and also from M&GN sheds, No.6028 being at King's Lynn from June 1938. The lamp iron on top of the smokebox proved unsuitable for holding the white disc used for train type indication so a GER type iron was added on the smokebox door.

All had, and retained, a steam brake on the engine and tender combined with a vacuum ejector for train working. Before a superheater was put in, the ejector exhaust pipe was through the boiler (*see* page 51).After superheating, the pipe was external on the right hand side adjacent to the handrail. A small drainpipe was added just at the rear of the smokebox.

6036 cont./
SHEDS:
Lincoln 26/5/22.
Immingham 21/8/24.
New Holland 11/1/30.
Immingham 24/4/30.
Trafford Park 10/2/38.

RENUMBERED:
1036c 3/11/23.
6036 4/7/25.
2320 allocated.

CONDEMNED: 3/1/46.
Cut up at Gorton.

_____

6037

Sharp Stewart 4847.

To traffic 5/1902.

REPAIRS:
Gor. 15/4—28/5/10.**G.**
Gor. 13/11/15—20/5/16.**G.**
Rebuilt with 5' 0" boiler.
Gor. 16/12/22—3/3/23.**G.**
Gor. 28/11/25—3/4/26.**G.**
Gor. 3/12/27—4/2/28.**G.**
Gor. 31/8—26/10/29.**G.**
Gor. 18/7—29/8/31.**G.**
Gor. 30/9—14/10/33.**G.**
Mech. lub. to cylinders.
Gor. 6—27/4/35.**G.**
To Part 2.
Gor. 3—24/10/36.**G.**
Gor. 29/5—12/6/37.**L.**
Gor. 15/10—12/11/38.**G.**
Gor. 30/3—18/5/40.**G.**
Gor. 14/5—20/6/42.**G.**
Gor. 14/2—11/3/44.**G.**
Gor. 23/2—16/3/46.**G.**
Gor. 29/11—20/12/47.**G.**

BOILERS:
   94 28/5/10.
1597 *(sup.)* 20/5/16.
  453 3/3/23.
1784 3/4/26.
  392 26/10/29.
  291 29/8/31.
  411 14/10/33.
  156 27/4/35.
  845 24/10/36.
3847 12/11/38.
  816 11/3/44.
3860 16/3/46.
  704 20/12/47.

SHEDS:
Sheffield 26/5/22.
Annesley 21/5/24.
Colwick 2/4/28.
Annesley 16/5/29.
Colwick 24/7/29.
King's Lynn 22/6/37.
Brunswick 28/3/39.

RENUMBERED:
  6037 3/4/26.
  2321 28/7/46.
62321 5/3/49.

CONDEMNED: 10/10/49.
Cut up at Dukinfield.

_____

6038

Sharp Stewart 4964.

To traffic 3/1903.

REPAIRS:
Gor. 10/10—5/12/08.**G.**
Gor. 18/4—4/10/14.**G.**
Rebuilt with 5' 0" boiler.
Gor. 28/1—4/3/22.**G.**
Gor. 27/10/23—12/1/24.**G.**
Gor. 31/10—31/12/25.**G.**
Gor. 18/6—13/8/27.**G.**
Gor. 20/10—15/12/28.**G.**
Gor. 30/8—11/10/30.**G.**
Gor. 19/3—16/4/32.**G.**
Gor. 10/3—5/5/34.**G.**
Gor. 25/1—8/2/36.**G.**
Gor. 18/7—8/8/36.**G.**
Gor. 18/9—23/10/37.**G.**
To Part 2.
Gor. 26/8—16/9/39.**G.**
Gor. 5—29/11/41.**G.**
Gor. 30/12/42—16/1/43.**L.**
Gor. 10/6—1/7/44.**G.**
Gor. 5—26/10/46.**G.**
Gor. 15—22/11/47.**L.**

BOILERS:
  321.
   98 5/12/08.
  413 *(sup.)* 4/10/14.
1624 4/3/22.
1427 12/1/24.
1665 11/10/30.
1684 16/4/32.
  118 5/5/34.
  386 8/2/36.
  939 23/10/37.
  696 16/9/39.
  658 29/11/41.
3844 1/7/44.

168 26/10/46.

SHEDS:
Annesley 14/5/20.
Colwick 2/4/28.
King's Lynn 13/7/38.
Yarmouth Beach 7/3/39.
March 11/8/43.
South Lynn 17/3/44.
Northwich 11/8/46.
Trafford Park 10/8/47.
Heaton Mersey 27/11/47.

RENUMBERED:
1038c 19/1/24.
6038 31/12/25.
2322 7/9/46.

CONDEMNED: 12/1/49.
Cut up at Dukinfield.

_____

6039

Sharp Stewart 4965.

To traffic 3/1903.

REPAIRS:
Gor. 6/7—12/10/12.**G.**
Gor. 23/12/16—17/2/17.**G.**
Gor. 4/2—27/5/22.**G.**
Rebuilt with 5' 0" boiler.
Gor. 24/5—16/8/24.**G.**
Gor. 17/4—24/7/26.**G.**
Gor. 28/4—9/6/28.**G.**
Gor. 24/5—26/7/30.**G.**
Gor. 9/7—20/8/32.**G.**
Gor. 10/3—14/4/34.**G.**
To Part 2.
Gor. 9—23/11/35.**G.**
To Part 1.
Gor. 5—31/12/36.**G.**
To Part 2.
Gor. 21/1—25/2/39.**G.**
Gor. 25/1—8/2/41.**G.**
Gor. 21/9—17/10/42.**G.**
Gor. 22/7—5/8/44.**G.**
Gor. 21/4/45.**L.**

BOILERS:
  322.
   82 12/10/12.
  885 17/2/17.
  413 *(sup.)* 27/5/22.
1665 16/8/24.
  391 26/7/30.
1825 20/8/32.
  168 14/4/34.
  276 23/11/35.
  156 31/12/36.

118 25/2/39.
845 8/2/41.
149 17/10/42.
658 5/8/44.

SHEDS:
Annesley 27/10/22.
Colwick 2/4/28.
Annesley 15/12/31.
Colwick 4/1/32.
Mexborough 15/6/37.
Trafford Park 25/2/39.
Brunswick 7/10/45.

RENUMBERED:
6039 16/8/24.
2323 allocated.

CONDEMNED: 3/1/46.
Cut up at Gorton.

_____

6040

Sharp Stewart 4966.

To traffic 3/1903.

REPAIRS:
Gor. 8/3—10/4/09.**G.**
Gor. 3—25/3/11.**G.**
Gor. 14/9/18—1/3/19.**G.**
Rebuilt with 5' 0" boiler.
Gor. 7/10—2/12/22.**G.**
Gor. 15/11/24—24/1/25.**G.**
Gor. 15/1—9/4/27.**G.**
Gor. 13/4—1/6/29.**G.**
Gor. 24/1—28/2/31.**G.**
Gor. 24/12/32—28/1/33.**G.**
Gor. 5—19/1/35.**G.**
To Part 2.
Gor. 10—24/4/37.**G.**
Tablet app. fitted.
Gor. 6—20/5/39.**G.**
Gor. 4—27/6/42.**G.**
Gor. 30/12/44—27/1/45.**G.**
Gor. 17/5—16/8/47.**G.**
Gor. 7/11/49. *Not repaired.*

BOILERS:
  323.
  885 10/4/09.
  325 25/3/11.
1428 *(sup.)* 1/3/19.
  413 24/1/25.
  168 28/2/31.
  774 28/1/33.
  410 19/1/35.
1780 24/4/37.
  156 20/5/39.
  704 27/6/42.

_____

WORKS CODES:- Bpk - Beyer, Peacock. Cow - Cowlairs. Dar - Darlington. Don - Doncaster. Efd - Eastfield. Ghd - Gateshead. Gor - Gorton. Inv - Inverurie. Str - Stratford. Wfd - Woodford.
REPAIR CODES:- **C/H** - Casual Heavy. **C/L** - Casual Light. **G** - General. **H** - Heavy. **H/I** - Heavy Intermediate. **L** - Light. **L/I** - Light Intermediate. **N/C** - Non-Classified.

In the period from February to June 1937, five, Nos.5112, 6013, 6021, 6040 and 6041, were transferred to work on the M&GN and Whittaker tablet exchanging apparatus was fitted to their tender at Gorton. No.6038 in July 1938 was also fitted as 6035 had been in May 1936, these two being shedded at King's Lynn. Gorton works.

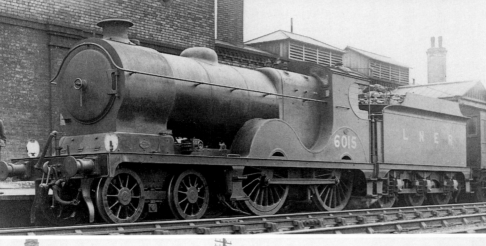

No.6015 working in the Peterborough area of the GE Section from 1937 to 1939, got an alteration made locally to its cab cut-out to give greater protection to the crew. It was the only one so noted.

Sanding was the usual GCR arrangement - steam applied ahead of the leading coupled wheels only. For running in reverse there were boxes at footplate level on the front of the tender with gravity feed.

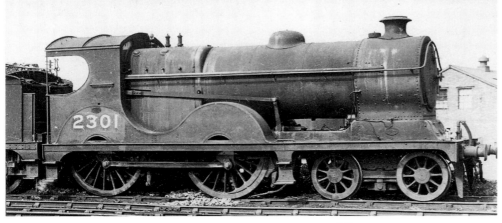

The mechanical lubricator was combined with an anti-carboniser for which the steam was taken from the rear of the smokebox on the right hand side.

(above) **None of this class was ever equipped with sightscreens on the cab side. Gorton works.**

(right) **Only the last ten engines came out with a 4000-gallon tender fitted with water scoop. By exchanging with early the C4 class and taking more modern tenders from later built J11 class, all D9's at Grouping had 4000 gallon tender with water pick-up apparatus. Most had solid coping with beading around the edge.**

(below) **Until August 1931, No.6033 had the tender built for C4 class No.5260 on which the four open coal rails had been retained with no attempt at plating them.**

6040 cont./
957 27/1/45.
719 16/8/47.

SHEDS:
Sheffield *at* 27/4/22.
Immingham 22/10/25.
Sheffield 23/12/25.
Retford 26/9/32.
Sheffield 28/11/32.
Peterborough East 26/11/35.
South Lynn 12/6/37.
March 2/10/37.
South Lynn 14/11/37.
King's Lynn 22/10/39.
South Lynn 14/2/40.
Stratford 19/12/45.
South Lynn 24/1/46.
Cambridge 19/6/46.
Brunswick 10/7/46.

RENUMBERED:
6040 24/1/25.
2324 28/7/46.
62324 19/3/49.

CONDEMNED: 7/11/49.
Cut up at Dukinfield.

_____

6041

Sharp Stewart 4967.

To traffic 3/1903.

REPAIRS:
Gor. 10/2—3/3/10.**G.**
Gor. 19/10/12—28/6/13.**G.**
Rebuilt with 5' 0" boiler.
Gor. 20/8/21—25/2/22.**G.**
Gor. 9/2—12/4/24.**G.**
Gor. 25/9—11/12/26.**G.**
Gor. 2/2—9/3/29.**G.**
Gor. 28/3—25/4/31.**G.**
Gor. 18/11—2/12/33.**G.**
Gor. 21/9—12/10/35.**G.**
Gor. 24/4—15/5/37.**G.**
To Part 2.
Tablet app. fitted.
Gor. 21/1—11/2/39.**L.**
Gor. 12/8—16/9/39.**G.**
Gor. 24/7—30/8/41.**G.**
Gor. 15/12/41—3/1/42.**H.**
Gor. 10—26/9/42.**L.**
Gor. 11—28/8/43.**G.**
Gor. 29/9—20/10/45.**G.**
Gor. 22—29/12/45.**L.**
Gor. 1—15/6/46.**L.**
Steam chest fracture.
Gor. 6—13/9/47.**L.**
Frame fracture.
Gor. 15/11/47.**L.**
After collision.

Gor. 1/5—5/6/48.**G.**
Gor. 15/10/49.**C/L.**
Tender bottom fracture.

BOILERS:
324.
  81 3/3/10.
138 *(sup.)* 28/6/13.
941 25/2/22.
366 25/4/31.
1905 2/12/33.
1597 12/10/35.
846 15/5/37.
3844 16/9/39.
653 30/8/41.
3846 28/8/43.
174 20/10/45.
939 5/6/48.

SHEDS:
Sheffield 16/6/22.
Peterborough East 29/6/36.
South Lynn 29/5/37.
March 2/10/37.
South Lynn 12/6/38.
Yarmouth Beach 24/9/38.
March 25/7/43.
Gorton 3/8/45.
Trafford Park 24/8/45.
Heaton Mersey 9/1/49.

RENUMBERED:
6041 12/4/24.
2325 12/6/46.
62325 5/6/48.

CONDEMNED: 6/2/50.
Cut up at Gorton 11/3/50.

_____

6042

Sharp Stewart 4968.

To traffic 3/1903.

REPAIRS:
Gor. 3/9—29/10/10.**G.**
Gor. 27/1—17/3/17.**G.**
Gor. 20/3—8/5/20.**G.**
Gor. 7/10—25/11/22.**G.**
19" P.V. cylinders fitted.
Gor. 21/6—27/9/24.**G.**
Gor. 2/10/26—8/1/27.**G.**
Rebuilt with 5' 0" boiler.
Gor. 29/9—17/11/28.**G.**
Gor. 8/11—13/12/30.**G.**
Gor. 29/4—13/5/33.**G.**
Gor. 16—30/3/35.**G.**
Gor. 6—27/3/37.**G.**
To Part 2.
Don. 22/11/38—11/3/39.**L.**
After derailment.

BOILERS:
325.
393 29/10/10.
321 17/3/17.
184 8/5/20.
596 *(sup.)* 8/1/27.
396 13/5/33.
1780 30/3/35.
806 27/3/37.

SHEDS:
Sheffield.
Retford.
Sheffield 5/8/28.
Peterborough East 29/6/36.
March 1/5/39.

RENUMBERED:
6042 27/9/24.

CONDEMNED: 7/7/39.
Cut up at Gorton.

_____

5104

QUEEN ALEXANDRA

Vulcan 1917.

To traffic 3/1904.

REPAIRS:
Gor. 19/1—23/3/07.**G.**
Rebuilt with 5' 0" sat. boiler.
Gor. 23/10/20—5/2/21.**G.**
Gor. 20/1—2/6/23.**G.**
19" P.V. cylinders fitted.
Gor. 16/5—3/10/25.**G.**
Gor. 9/7—27/8/27.**G.**
Gor. 19/1—9/3/29.**G.**
Gor. 15/11—13/12/30.**G.**
Gor. 12/11—3/12/32.**G.**
Gor. 7—28/7/34.**G.**
Gor. 22/2—28/3/36.**G.**
Alt to 13' 0" gauge.
Gor. 29/5—12/6/37.**G.**
Gor. 9—23/7/38.**G.**
Gor. 25/5—22/6/40.**G.**
Gor. 28/11—19/12/42.**G.**
Gor. 6/9/44. *Not repaired.*

BOILERS:
885.
552 23/3/07.
1694 *(sup.)* 2/6/23.
1422 3/10/25.
253 13/12/30.
772 3/12/32.
1795 28/7/34.
772 28/3/36.
3842 12/6/37.
174 23/7/38.
806 22/6/40.

119 19/12/42.

SHEDS:
Retford 19/5/22.
Sheffield 13/11/24.
Retford *by* 5/1/30.
Sheffield 29/9/30.
Retford 5/1/31.
Sheffield 21/9/32.
Immingham 18/10/32.
Lincoln 19/10/32.
Brunswick 15/5/33.
Trafford Park 21/5/44.

RENUMBERED:
5104 3/10/25.
2326 allocated.

CONDEMNED: 6/9/44.
Cut up at Gorton.

_____

5105

Vulcan 1918.

To traffic 3/1904.

REPAIRS:
Gor. 21/11—26/12/08.**G.**
Gor. 14/3—15/8/14.**G.**
Rebuilt with 5' 0" sat. boiler.
Gor. 25/12/15—29/1/16.**G.**
Reverted to 4' 9" boiler.
Gor. 12/3—16/4/21.**G.**
Gor. 14/7—17/11/23.**G.**
Rebuilt with 5' 0" boiler.
Gor. 3/10—19/12/25.**G.**
Gor. 3/12/27—4/2/28.**G.**
Gor. 9/11—21/12/29.**G.**
Gor. 26/3—23/4/32.**G.**
Gor. 12/5—2/6/34.**G.**
Gor. 12—26/12/36.**G.**
To Part 2.
Gor. 26/11—24/12/38.**G.**
Gor. 12/7—2/8/41.**G.**
Gor. 15/9—2/10/43.**G.**
Gor. 30/6/45. *Not repaired.*

BOILERS:
886.
  83 26/12/08.
677 15/8/14.
451 29/1/16.
1699 *(sup.)* 17/11/23.
325 23/4/32.
119 2/6/34.
800 26/12/36.
653 24/12/38.
  91 2/8/41.
844 2/10/43.

SHEDS:
Retford 19/5/22.

No.6016's tender had been built in 1907 for J11 No.5286 and by Grouping it had been plated on the inside of the rails. It remained with No.6016 until March 1945 and was with 2329 (ex-5107) from November 1946 to August 1948.

No.6014's tender was a rebuilt version of 6080's original and on which a coping, without beading, had been fitted, to the outside of the coal rails. 6014 kept this tender until October 1947 and it then went to 2322 (6038) from November 1947 to December 1948 and to 2314 (6030) from December 1948 to May 1949.

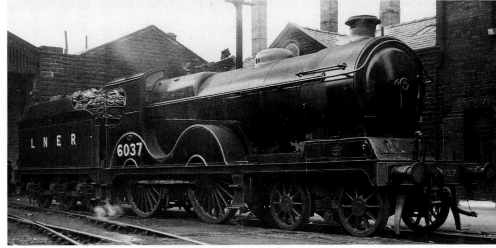

No.6037's tender came from No.6033 in August 1931 and the open coal rails had been plated on the outside. This tender (No.5260) was with 6037 to October 1943 and then served another fifteen years with a J11 engine. Note the spoked handwheel for operating the water pick-up apparatus.

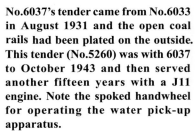

In 1938 it was decided to remove the water pick-up apparatus from all classes no longer employed on runs requiring its use. Only a few had been dealt with before the war brought this intention to a halt. From 1945 however most of D9 class had the pick-up removed, as shown by the absence of operating wheel. Manchester (Central) loco yard.

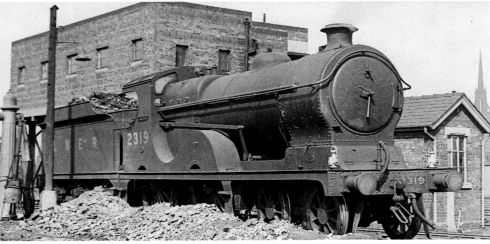

(above) **From 1929 numbers were moved from tender to cab and, as shown in the illustration of No.6037 on the previuos page, were placed inside the brass beading of the rear splasher. Six of the class, Nos.5105, 5109, 6017, 6031, 6035 and 6036 are known to have had their beading removed, but initially this had no effect on the number position.**

(left) **By 1935 it had been realised that on engines without the beading, the cab numbering could be on the same level as the tender lettering and this was made standard for those concerned. This higher number position caused the small numberplate to be fixed below the transfers instead of above them as was customary.**

In GC ownership all forty had fully lined green painting, with the coat-of-arms on the leading splasher and between the two words on the tender.

5105 cont./
Sheffield *by* 9/24.
Mexborough 9/4/36.
Barnsley 8/12/39.
Trafford Park 5/2/44.

RENUMBERED:
105c 24/11/23.
5105 19/12/25.
2327 allocated.

CONDEMNED: 25/6/45.
Cut up at Gorton.

5106

Vulcan 1919.

To traffic 4/1904.

REPAIRS:
Gor. 17/1—13/6/14.**G.**
Rebuilt with 5' 0" boiler.
Gor. 2/7—20/8/21.**G.**
Gor. 22/9—15/12/23.**G.**
Gor. 25/4—18/7/25.**G.**
Gor. 26/2—30/4/27.**G.**
Gor. 15/12/28—16/2/29.**G.**
Gor. 15/11—20/12/30.**G.**
Gor. 19/11—10/12/32.**G.**
Gor. 14/7—4/8/34.**G.**
Gor. 4—25/4/36.**G.**
Gor. 11/12/37—15/1/38.**G.**
To Part 2.
Gor. 27/4—1/6/40.**G.**
Gor. 26/6—25/7/42.**G.**
Gor. 30/6—24/7/43.**L.**
Gor. 10—28/10/44.**G.**
Gor. 23/2/46.**L.**
Tender change.
Gor. 11/1/47. *Not repaired.*

BOILERS:
887.
185 *(sup.)* 13/6/14.
1419 15/12/23.
281 16/2/29.
149 10/12/32.
325 4/8/34.
1795 25/4/36.
799 15/1/38.
936 25/7/42.
799 28/10/44.

SHEDS:
Sheffield 7/1/21.
Retford 30/4/24.
Sheffield 18/10/28.
Retford 4/4/29.
Sheffield 17/10/30.
Retford 23/1/31.
Sheffield 26/9/32.
Retford 20/12/32.
Sheffield 10/3/36.

Retford 30/4/36.
Brunswick 11/9/42.
Walton-on-the-Hill 7/11/43.

RENUMBERED:
106c 5/1/24.
5106 18/7/25.
2328 18/8/46.

CONDEMNED: 20/3/47.
Cut up at Gorton.

5107

Vulcan 1920.

To traffic 4/1904.

REPAIRS:
Wfd. 24/6—29/7/10.**G.**
Gor. 12/5—24/6/11.**G.**
Gor. 22/9—15/12/17.**G.**
Gor. 5/8—28/10/22.**G.**
Gor. 10/5—13/9/24.**G.**
Rebuilt with 5' 0" boiler.
Gor. 25/10—29/11/24.**G.**
Gor. 5/3—23/4/27.**G.**
Gor. 13/4—18/5/29.**G.**
Gor. 18/4—16/5/31.**G.**
Gor. 24/6—8/7/33.**G.**
To Part 2.
Gor. 15—29/2/36.**G.**
Gor. 30/10—20/11/37.**G.**
Gor. 20/1—10/2/40.**G.**
Gor. 13—27/3/43.**G.**
Gor. 28/7—25/8/45.**G.**
Gor. 2—30/11/46.**G.**
Gor. 17/5/47.**L.**
Frame cracked.

BOILERS:
888.
76 29/7/10.
893 24/6/11.
393 15/12/17.
557 *(sup.)* 13/9/24.
1669 16/5/31.
808 8/7/33.
947 29/2/36.
810 20/11/37.
3846 10/2/40.
3842 27/3/43.
3859 25/8/45.
714 30/11/46.

SHEDS:
Retford 29/12/22.
Sheffield *by* 31/1/24.
Mexborough 15/4/36.
Trafford Park 5/10/44.

RENUMBERED:
5107 13/9/24.
2329 11/8/46.

CONDEMNED: 26/2/49.
Cut up at Dukinfield.

5108

Vulcan 1921.

To traffic 4/1904.

REPAIRS:
Gor. 24/4—12/6/09.**G.**
Gor. 13/5—24/6/11.**G.**
Gor. 8/3—4/10/13.**G.**
Rebuilt with 5' 0" boiler.
Gor. 11/6—16/7/21.**G.**
Gor. 6/10/23—12/1/24.**G.**
Gor. 30/1—17/4/26.**G.**
Gor. 24/3—5/5/28.**G.**
Gor. 8/2—15/3/30.**G.**
Gor. 26/3—23/4/32.**G.**
Gor. 12/5—2/6/34.**G.**
To Part 2.
Gor. 4—25/7/36.**G.**
Gor. 29/8—26/9/36.**L.**
Gor. 11/3—1/4/39.**G.**
Gor. 22/10—15/11/41.**G.**
Gor. 6—20/5/44.**G.**
Gor. 10/3/45.**L.**
After collision.
Gor. 13/4—11/5/46.**G.**
Gor. 14/2—6/3/48.**G.**
Gor. 15/8/49. *Not repaired.*

BOILERS:
889.
85 12/6/09.
91 24/6/11.
121 *(sup.)* 4/10/13.
1424 16/7/21.
278 5/5/28.
1665 23/4/32.
171 2/6/34.
392 25/7/36.
658 1/4/39.
3844 15/11/41.
3851 20/5/44.
3847 11/5/46.
3860 6/3/48.

SHEDS:
Sheffield 18/11/21.
Retford 21/9/32.
Sheffield 20/12/32.
Retford 29/11/37.
Sheffield 29/1/38.
Mexborough 1/4/39.
Trafford Park 5/10/44.
Brunswick 15/10/44.
Trafford Park 3/12/44.

RENUMBERED:
108c 12/1/24.
5108 17/4/26.
2330 11/8/46.

ᴇ**2330** 6/3/48.
62330 29/1/49.

CONDEMNED: 15/8/49.
Cut up at Dukinfield.

5109

Vulcan 1922.

To traffic 4/1904.

REPAIRS:
Gor. 7/5—2/7/10.**G.**
Gor. 2/9—21/10/11.**G.**
Gor. 6/12/13—16/5/14.**G.**
Rebuilt with 5' 0" boiler.
Gor. 16/7/21—1/4/22.**G.**
Gor. 31/5—9/8/24.**G.**
Gor. 22/1—19/3/27.**G.**
Gor. 31/3—19/5/28.**G.**
Gor. 27/4—1/6/29.**G.**
Gor. 6/6—4/7/31.**G.**
Gor. 24/6—19/8/33.**G.**
Mech. lub. to cylinders.
Gor. 21/4—5/5/34.**G.**
Gor. 14—31/12/35.**G.**
To Part 2.
Gor. 15/1—5/2/38.**G.**
Gor. 21/5—25/6/38.**L.**
Frame cracked.
Gor. 23/7—6/8/38.**L.**
After collision.
Gor. 3—24/8/40.**G.**
Gor. 29/8—12/9/42.**G.**
Gor. 12/9—7/10/44.**G.**
Gor. 28/9/46. *Not repaired.*

BOILERS:
890.
892 2/7/10.
1153 21/10/11.
81 *(sup.)* 16/5/14.
281 19/3/27.
1425 19/5/28.
386 4/7/31.
1669 19/8/33.
942 31/12/35.
844 5/2/38.
149 24/8/40.
799 12/9/42.
986 7/10/44.

SHEDS:
Sheffield 7/1/21.
Immingham 21/10/25.
New Holland *after* 21/5/27.
Immingham 22/2/29.
New Holland 6/6/35.
Lincoln 17/8/35.
King's Lynn 5/5/36.
Brunswick 26/5/39.

5109 cont./
RENUMBERED:
5109 9/8/24.
2331 26/1/46.

CONDEMNED: 28/9/46.
Cut up at Gorton.

5110

KING GEORGE V

Vulcan 1923.

To traffic 5/1904.

REPAIRS:
Gor. ?/?—11/5/07.**G.**
Altered to 5' 0" sat. boiler.
Gor. 4/5—10/8/18.**G.**
Reverted to 4' 9" boiler.
Gor. 4/12/20—1/1/21.**G.**
Gor. 17/2—22/9/23.**G.**
*19" P.V. cylinders and
5' 0" boiler fitted.*
Gor. 31/10/25—30/1/26.**G.**
Gor. 7/1—25/2/28.**G.**
Gor. 23/11—31/12/29.**G.**
Gor. 5—26/3/32.**G.**
Gor. 20/1—10/2/34.**G.**
To Part 2.
Gor. 29/2—4/4/36.**G.**
Gor. 4/6—9/7/38.**G.**
Gor. 3/2—2/3/40.**G.**
Gor. 21/2/42. *Not repaired.*

BOILERS:
891.
235 11/5/07.
1153 10/8/18.
319 1/1/21.
1194 *(sup.)* 22/9/23.
1795 31/12/29.
1644 26/3/32.
816 10/2/34.
174 4/4/36.
3841 9/7/38.

SHEDS:
Retford 19/5/22.
Brunswick *by* 12/22.
Gorton 17/3/25.
Brunswick 31/3/25.
Annesley 14/2/26.
Sheffield 7/4/26.
Staveley 16/6/36.
Sheffield 31/7/36.
Trafford Park 19/11/38.

RENUMBERED:
110c 13/10/23.
5110 30/1/26.

CONDEMNED: 3/3/42.
Cut up at Gorton.

5111

Vulcan 1924.

To traffic 5/1904.

REPAIRS:
Gor. 21/12/09—29/1/10.**G.**
Gor. 6/5—11/11/16.**G.**
Rebuilt with 5' 0" boiler.
Gor. 21/4—18/10/21.**H.**
Gor. 2/6—29/9/23.**G.**
Gor. 18/7—12/12/25.**G.**
Gor. 14/4—26/5/28.**G.**
Gor. 23/11/29—11/1/30.**G.**
Gor. 12/3—9/4/32.**G.**
Gor. 26/5—16/6/34.**G.**
Gor. 13—27/6/36.**G.**
To Part 2.
Gor. 26/3—23/4/38.**G.**
Gor. 6/1—8/6/40.**G.**
Gor. 5—20/3/43.**G.**
Gor. 17/3—7/4/45.**G.**
Gor. 28/9—26/10/46.**G.**
Gor. 1—8/11/47.**L.**
Gor. 7/8—4/9/48.**G.**

BOILERS:
892.
90 29/1/10.
1638 *(sup.)* 11/11/16.
1562 12/12/25.
1795 9/4/32.
1665 16/6/34.
783 27/6/36.
3845 23/4/38.
806 20/3/43.
3861 7/4/45.
968 26/10/46.
984 4/9/48.

SHEDS:
Sheffield 7/1/21.
Retford 27/3/33.
Sheffield 4/5/33.
Retford 6/7/36.
Sheffield 29/1/37.
Retford 29/10/37.
Sheffield 28/1/38.
Trafford Park 21/11/38.
Brunswick 16/9/39.

RENUMBERED:
5111 12/12/25.
2332 11/8/46.
62332 4/9/48.

CONDEMNED: 5/9/49.
Cut up at Dukinfield.

5112

Vulcan 1925.

To traffic 5/1904.

REPAIRS:
Gor. 25/11/10—18/1/11.**G.**
Gor. 25/5—26/10/18.**G.**
19" P.V. cylinders. fitted.
Gor. 23/10—4/12/20.**G.**
Gor. 19/8—21/10/22.**G.**
Gor. 16/2—24/5/24.**G.**
Rebuilt with 5' 0" boiler.
Gor. 7/11/25—16/1/26.**G.**
Gor. 22/10—17/12/27.**G.**
Gor. 7/12/29—18/1/30.**G.**
Gor. 7/5—11/6/32.**G.**
Gor. 2—23/3/35.**G.**
Mech. lub. to cylinders.
Gor. 20/2—13/3/37.**G.**
To Part 2.
Tablet app. fitted.
Gor. 3—17/2/40.**G.**
Gor. 25/9—16/10/43.**G.**
Gor. 22/12/45.**L.**
Tender change.
Gor. 21/6—2/8/47.**G.**
Gor. 24/7—7/8/48.**L.**
Frame fractured.

BOILERS:
893.
888 28/1/11.
324 26/10/18.
1644 *(sup.)* 24/5/24.
1194 18/1/30.
718 11/6/32.
806 23/3/35.
210 13/3/37.
939 17/2/40.
810 16/10/43.
957 2/8/47.

SHEDS:
Mexborough. 8/4/21.
Retford. 12/1/23.
Sheffield 5/6/24.
Staveley 26/9/32.
Sheffield 7/4/33.
Retford 8/1/36.
Sheffield 4/5/36.
Retford 31/8/36.
Sheffield 12/10/36.
South Lynn 13/3/37.
King's Lynn 22/1/38.
South Lynn 12/6/38.
King's Lynn 28/9/38.
Yarmouth Beach 19/1/39.
King's Lynn 12/3/39.
South Lynn 24/5/39.
March 10/3/40.
South Lynn 9/6/40.
March 9/2/41.

South Lynn 5/8/43.
Brunswick 9/7/46.

RENUMBERED:
5112 24/5/24.
2333 27/1/46.
62333 7/8/48.

CONDEMNED: 12/12/49.
*Into Gor. for cut up 17/12/49
but cut up at Dukinfield.*

5113

Vulcan 1926.

To traffic 6/1904.

REPAIRS:
Gor. 3/9—8/10/10.**G.**
Gor. 2/3—5/10/18.**G.**
*19" P.V. cylinders and
5' 0" saturated boiler fitted.*
Gor. 6/11/20—29/1/21.**G.**
Gor. 27/1—19/5/23.**G.**
Superheated boiler fitted.
Gor. 2/1—26/6/26.**G.**
Gor. 22/9—3/11/28.**G.**
Gor. 15—22/6/29.**L.**
Gor. 28/6—16/8/30.**G.**
Gor. 2—16/4/32.**G.**
Gor. 28/10—11/11/33.**G.**
Gor. 23/11—14/12/35.**G.**
To Part 2.
Gor. 26/6—24/7/37.**G.**
Gor. 7/6/39. *Not repaired.*

BOILERS:
894.
324 8/10/10.
235 5/10/18.
1684 *(sup.)* 19/5/23.
718 26/6/26.
1562 16/4/32.
1694 11/11/33.
843 14/12/35.
936 24/7/37.

SHEDS:
Lincoln.
Peterborough East 29/6/36.
March 30/4/39.

RENUMBERED:
5113 26/6/26.

CONDEMNED: 7/6/39.
Cut up at Gorton.

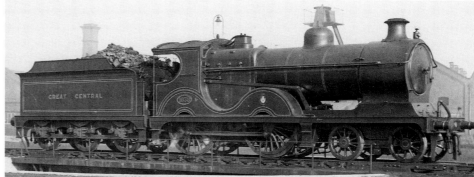

One effect of the 1914-1918 war was that the coat-of-arms was omitted from the tender but its use had been restored before the LNER took over.

The first D9 to get LNER livery was No.1026, ex paint shop on 10th February 1923 and it kept the GCR coat-of-arms on the splasher, whilst its L.&N.E.R. lettering was only 6in. high. No.1027, ex paint shop (3rd March 1923) was the only other to keep its GCR arms but that engine had 7½ in. initials. Four others, Nos.1028 (21st April 9123), 1037 (12th May 1923), 1018 (26th May 1923) and 1034 (2nd June 1923) had the ampersand and full points included in their 7½ in. initials, which were then discarded.

Two engines, Nos.113 (7th July 1923) and 104 (28th July 1923) were the first with LNER only, and were the only two in this style.

Nos.1019 and 1035 were the next (ex paint shop 1st September 1923) and these had the suffix C to the number. Eight others also came out with the suffix: 1023 (22nd September 1923), 110 (13th October 1923), 1036 (3rd November 1923), 1016 (10th November 1923), 105 (24th November 1923), 106 (5th January 1924), 108 (12th January 1924) and 1038 (19th January 1924).

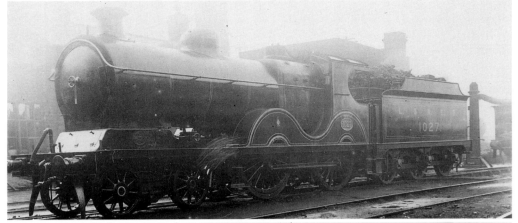

At some date not recorded, No.1027 had suffix C added, probably at its shed, because it did not visit works during the period September 1923 to January 1924 when the suffix was being put on.

No.1034, was in Gorton works for a light repair 16th February to 29th March 1924. When ex paint shop on 12th April 1924 the tender number and the large GC style plate on the cab had been changed to 6034.

Nos.6017 and 6032, ex paint shop on 2nd February 1924 were the first to get 1924 numbering and they, together with 6024 (9th February 1924), 5112 (31st May 1924) and 6041 (21st June 1924) were provided with the GC large brass cab number plate. The standard style began with 6033 ex paint shop on 12th July 1924 and it was then used until green painting was cancelled by the June 1928 economies. All the dates quoted in this caption, excepting No.6024, are ex paint shop and not 'ex works'. No.6024's date is ex works so perhaps that engine did not receive a repaint.

The change to black with single red lining first took effect on No.6020 (14th July 1928) and until April 1929 the number remained on the tender. At least eighteen were put into this style.

The maker's works plate was fitted on the frame below the smokebox, and was quite distinct from the LNER number plate on the cab. This shows the Sharp, Stewart type. Sheffield Neepsend shed.

The Vulcan Foundry plates were also elliptical but were noticeably deeper. Sheffield Neepsend shed.

The majority managed to keep their maker's plates to withdrawal, but Nos.6019, 6042, 5104, 5110, 5112 and 5113 are known to have lost them, and by 1925 in at least three cases.

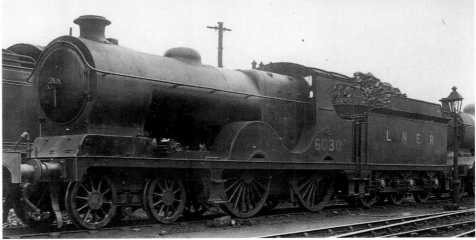

All duly went into black with single red lining and with number on the cab side. The company initials were then made 12in. in place of 7½in.

From March 1938 their classification was applied to the front buffer beam.

From November 1941 the lining was no longer applied, and from July 1942 only NE was put on the tender.

From January 1946 LNER was restored and in that year the survivors were renumbered. Gorton still had shaded transfers available when they sent out No.2318 on 15th November 1947 after its last general repair. Manchester (Central) loco yard.

No.2312 received shaded numerals on the cab and front buffer beam when ex works on 4th January 1947 from a general repair. In May 1948 it exchanged tenders with 2313 which had got BRITISH RAILWAYS put on in March 1948. Brunswick shed.

The LNER in shaded transfers remained on 2318's tender to withdrawal in November 1949. The engine had its BR number 62318 put on at its shed on 5th February 1949 when painted, unshaded correct Gill sans figures were applied. Note that no smokebox numberplate was fitted and that the buffer beam number was painted over. Trafford Park shed.

With only three exceptions unlined black continued in use to withdrawal. Although the splasher beading remained on most, it was painted over but the number was still put inside it. For 62301, ex works on 3rd July 1948 after a general repair, Gorton used 12in. painted numbers but with modified Gill sans figures and no smokebox plate was fitted. Gorton works.

When Gorton dealt with 62315 on 26th June 1948 they were able to paint the 12in. numbers on the same level as the tender letters because as 6031 this was one which had lost its splasher beading. Note that the smokebox plate was fitted and this - also the cab - had modified 6. Manchester (Central).

No.62300, ex Gorton on 20th March 1948, was about the first to have 6xxxx BR number. Whilst the figures were 12in. only 8in. tender letters were then used. Trafford Park shed.

In August/September 1948 Gorton gave full BR lining of red, cream and grey to just three D9 class at general repairs. Each had the splasher beading removed so that the cab number could match the tender lettering, both now being 10in. high. Ex works on 21st August 1948, No.62313 had a modified 6 both on cab side and smokebox plate.

When 62332 was ex works on 4th September 1948, it had been treated similarly except that on the cab correct Gill sans was painted. The smokebox plate however had already been cast with the modified 6.

(above) A week later on 11th September 1948, No.62317 was ex works just like 62332 but this was the last D9 to get such favoured painting. Trafford Park shed.

(right) When 62307 came out on 25th September 1948 from a general repair it was without any lining despite being a named engine (ex 6021 QUEEN MARY). The splasher beading was not taken off and the number with correct 6 was inserted. The smokebox plate however had the modified 6. Gorton works.

Three of the class were cut up at Darlington, Nos.62301 and 62312 on 17th June 1950 and 62305 on 14th October 1950, probably to see if further use of their boilers could be made. Those from Nos.62301 and 62305 were cut up with the engines but No.62312's boiler was used on Class A5. Darlington scrapyard.

Whilst at Lincoln 6030 was used to and from York for their portion of the Harwich boat train and here is leaving York with the 3.40pm ex York in 1932. Presumably the four-coach G.N. articulated set would be detached at Doncaster or it may be returning to Lincolnshire after repairs at York carriage works. Note also the GN six-wheeled coach. The engine left Lincoln on 6th June 1935 for New Holland, went on 31st March 1939 to Immingham, then on 24th March 1941 to Retford and on 20th May 1941 to New England. There on 2nd June 1941 it was nominated for M&GN line duty. It had one more transfer, to Stockport on 19th December 1945. They changed it to 2314 on 28th July 1946 and also to 62314 on 12th February 1949 before it was withdrawn on 9th May 1949, still with LNER on tender.

Numbered 6031 from 16th August 1924, this engine worked from Sheffield and here at Dringhouses on 4th October 1927 has just left York on a Newcastle to Swansea train. It went to Staveley on 26th September 1932 but back to Sheffield on 27th March 1933. On 9th March 1935 it moved to Norwich; 25th November 1935 to Peterborough East; 30th April 1939 to King's Lynn; 19th June 1939 to Cambridge and 31st May 1942 to March. 26th July 1946 saw its return to the GC at Liverpool where on 1st September 1946 they changed it to 2315. Ex works on 26th June 1948 it was 62315 and it was withdrawn on 18th July 1949.

By 1920 there had been changes. Element protection was by Robinson's combined blower and steam circulating valve, with a header discharge valve on the left-hand side of the smokebox. The mechanical lubrication had been removed and replaced by Robinson's Intensifore type. The front-end heater connection had been taken off some, but not all. The header discharge valve was still being used to 1926, No.5433 having it to September (*see* page 84, bottom). But another change had begun - 5430's boiler, built in 1915 was then fitted with Ramsbottom type safety valves, but when put on this D10 in January 1924 the mounting was adapted to take two Ross 'pop' valves. Neasden shed.

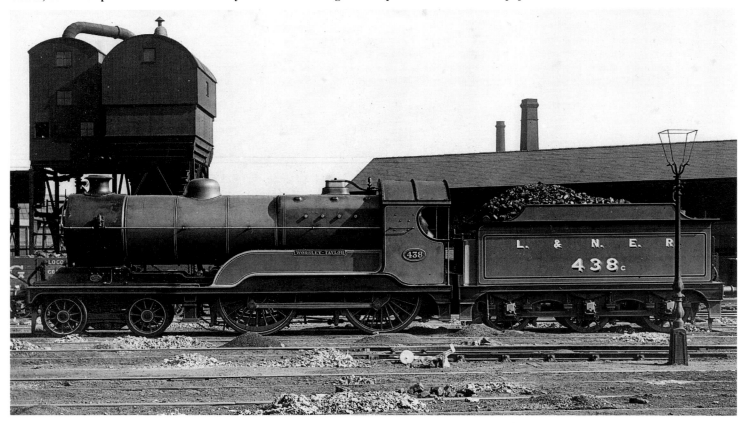

Generous provision was made for washout purposes. On the left hand side of the firebox four large plugs were fitted and on the shoulder were three handholes.

CLASS D 10

5429

PRINCE HENRY

Gorton.

To traffic 8/1913.

REPAIRS:
Gor. 19/3—21/5/21.**G.**
New cylinders.
Gor. 28/7—10/11/23.**G.**
Gor. 19/7—16/8/24.**G.**
Gor. 14/2—2/5/25.**G.**
Gor. 23—30/5/25.**L.**
Gor. 6/8—15/10/27.**G.**
New cylinders.
Gor. 21/9—19/10/29.**G.**
Gor. 25/10—29/11/30.**G.**
Gor. 14—28/3/31.**L.**
Gor. 12/3—16/4/32.**G.**
Gor. 18/11—16/12/33.**G.**
Gor. 6—20/7/35.**G.**
Gor. 13/2—27/3/37.**G.**
T.A.B. valves fitted.
Gor. 25/6—9/7/38.**L.**
Gor. 1—29/4/39.**G.**
Gor. 3—22/11/41.**G.**
Gor. 21/2—18/3/44.**G.**
Gor. 21/10—4/11/44.**L.**
Gor. 20/10—17/11/45.**G.**
New cylinders.
Gor. 23/8—27/9/47.**G.**
Gor. 27/8—24/9/49.**G.**
Gor. 15/12/51—19/1/52.**G.**

BOILERS:
1552.
1557 21/5/21.
1575 15/10/27.
997 19/10/29.
1890 29/11/30.
331 16/4/32.
614 16/12/33.
334 20/7/35.
3105 27/3/37.
687 29/4/39.
3116 22/11/41.
3107 18/3/44.
3112 17/11/45.
3121 27/9/47.
586 24/9/49.
22014 19/1/52.

SHEDS:
Neasden 5/8/21.
Annesley 26/1/23.
Gorton 10/3/23.
Neasden 3/6/25.
Gorton 23/10/27.
Sheffield 3/7/36.

Mexborough 25/2/40.
Darnall 10/8/43.
Northwich 27/11/47.

RENUMBERED:
429c 10/11/23.
5429 16/8/24.
2650 20/11/46.
62650 12/3/49.

CONDEMNED: 15/2/54.
Into Gor. for cut up 20/2/54.

5430

PURDON VICCARS

Gorton.

To traffic 9/1913.

REPAIRS:
Gor. 27/9—20/12/19.**G.**
Gor. 13/8—12/11/21.**G.**
Gor. 13/10/23—5/1/24.**G.**
Gor. 27/6—19/9/25.**G.**
Gor. 26/2—30/4/27.**G.**
Gor. 3/11—15/12/28.**G.**
Gor. 27/9—22/11/30.**G.**
New cylinders.
Gor. 3/6—22/7/33.**G.**
Gor. 13/7—10/8/35.**G.**
Gor. 24/4—10/5/37.**G.**
T.A.B. valves fitted.
Gor. 11/3—15/4/39.**G.**
Gor. 26/10—23/11/40.**G.**
New cylinders.
Gor. 4—19/6/43.**G.**
Gor. 22/9—17/11/45.**G.**
Gor. 16/8—27/9/47.**G.**
Gor. 26/6—14/8/48.**L.**
Frame fracture.
Gor. 23/7—13/8/49.**G.**
Gor. 24/6—1/7/50.**C/L.**
Gor. 19/5—9/6/51.**G.**

BOILERS:
1553.
1813 20/12/19.
988 5/1/24.
611 30/4/27.
1813 15/12/28.
494 22/11/30.
614 10/8/35.
593 10/5/37.
586 15/4/39.
3115 23/11/40.
683 19/6/43.
3115 17/11/45.
3116 27/9/47.

593 13/8/49.
22009 9/6/51.

SHEDS:
Gorton 22/7/21.
Annesley 16/2/23.
Gorton 10/3/23.
Neasden 21/3/24.
Gorton 20/5/33.
Neasden 22/7/33.
Woodford 12/6/34.
Neasden 30/6/34.
Sheffield 2/7/36.
Doncaster 12/12/41.
Langwith Jct. 15/2/43.
Darnall 29/8/43.
Trafford Park 27/11/47.
Brunswick 9/10/49.
Northwich 22/5/50.

RENUMBERED:
430c 12/1/24.
5430 19/9/25.
2651 8/10/46.
62651 14/8/48.

CONDEMNED: 9/3/53.
Into Gor. for cut up 14/3/53.

5431

EDWIN A. BEAZLEY

Gorton.

To traffic 10/1913.

REPAIRS:
Gor. 1/5—5/6/20.**G.**
Gor. 5—26/3/21.**L.**
New cylinders.
Gor. 13/1—24/3/23.**G.**
Gor. 7/6—2/8/24.**G.**
Gor. 23/1—20/3/26.**G.**
Gor. 10/12/27—11/2/28.**G.**
Gor. 30/11/29—11/1/30.**G.**
Gor. 25/4—23/5/31.**G.**
Gor. 1—22/7/33.**G.**
Gor. 8/12/34—12/1/35.**G.**
T.A.B. valves fitted.
Gor. 13/3—10/4/37.**G.**
Gor. 15/7—5/8/39.**G.**
Gor. 10/3—11/4/42.**G.**
Gor. 20—27/11/43.**L.**
Gor. 1—22/4/44.**G.**
Gor. 2/6—21/7/45.**G.**
Gor. 20/4—15/6/46.**L.**
New cylinders.
Gor. 26/7—30/8/47.**G.**
Gor. 24—31/1/48.**L.**

Gor. 30/4—21/5/49.**G.**
Gor. 23/9—21/10/50.**G.**
Frames fractured.
Gor. 16/8—13/9/52.**L/I.**
Gor. 12/9/53.**C/L.**
Tender tank repair.
Gor. 5—12/12/53.**C/L.**

BOILERS:
1554.
1671 5/6/20.
1553 2/8/24.
612 20/3/26.
673 11/1/30.
1815 23/5/31.
1575 22/7/33.
593 12/1/35.
334 10/4/37.
614 5/8/39.
678 11/4/42.
3104 22/4/44.
3121 21/7/45.
3106 30/8/47.
682 21/5/49.
22001 21/10/50.

SHEDS:
Gorton 20/8/20.
Neasden 8/3/24.
Leicester 15/3/29.
Neasden 23/3/29.
Sheffield 25/7/32.
Copley Hill 28/10/32.
Sheffield 18/3/33.
Annesley 10/4/37.
Sheffield 7/1/39.
Mexborough 26/2/40.
Darnall 10/8/43.
Northwich 8/9/47.

RENUMBERED:
431c *"later in 1923"*
5431 2/8/24.
2652 8/10/46.
E2652 31/1/48.
62652 5/2/49.

CONDEMNED: 3/5/54.
Into Gor. for cut up 8/5/54.

5432

SIR EDWARD FRASER

Gorton.

To traffic 10/1913.

REPAIRS:
Gor. 5/8—30/9/16.**G.**

On the opposite side were the same number of openings but divided into two handholes and five plugs thus giving a staggered arrangement.

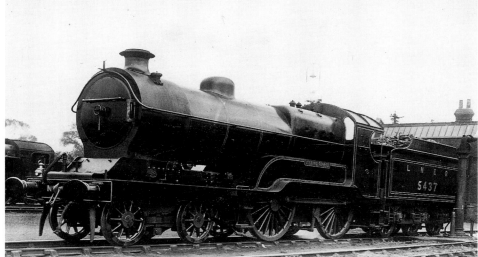

(left) In 1925 the simpler Gresley anti-vacuum valve began to be used for element protection and at first one was fitted at each end of the header. No.5431 also got that type, as did No.5436 in June 1931.

(left) Although the running plate was lifted adjacent to the coupled wheels, its edge was plated level with the valance. Although quite unnecessary, this plating was still there up to 1925/1926.

(opposite, top) During 1925 and 1926 the plating which handicapped access to the coupled wheel journals was removed. Other changes were to a single anti-vacuum valve behind the chimney and the replacement of the Intensifore lubrication by a Detroit or Wakefield Eureka sight feed type fitted in the cab. There were inclined feed pipes on both sides of the engine.

(opposite, bottom) Despite chimney alterations, no attempt was made to bring this class within the 13ft 0in. gauge. In March 1926, No.5431 was fitted with a 1ft 3in. 'plant pot' chimney but the dome and cab were still over 13ft 0in.

The 1ft 3in. 'plant pot' chimney was soon recognised as too short and a 1ft 5½in. variety was introduced. All had one or other of this type by 1930.

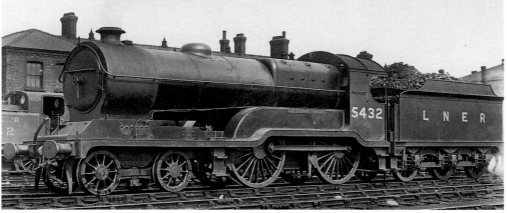

By 1933 the 'plant pot' type was being changed to a design more akin to the original but only 1ft 3in. tall. This became the standard used by all the class through to withdrawal. It was used independently of dome height.

The boiler was the same as used by D11 class, but when the D11 Part 2 engines were built for the Scottish Area in 1924 they had to have short domes to suit the NB gauge. To facilitate interchange, all subsequent boilers built for Classes D10 and D11 had the 4⅜in. shorter dome. Doncaster shed.

By Grouping, a smokebox ash ejector had been fitted and its steam supply entered at the rear of the box on the right hand side. Nottingham (Victoria).

(above) **By 1925 this steam entry point was found to be causing scouring of the front tube plate so it was changed to the front end of the box by fitting a longer pipe. Guide Bridge.**

(right) **Towards the end of the 1939-1945 war, or soon after, it was decided to dispense with the ash ejector and they were removed from all ten. Gorton shed.**

For sanding, the original fitting was steam applied (see page 85, top) ahead of the leading coupled wheels. For reverse running, the usual GC method of boxes at floor level on the front of the tender, with gravity feed was employed. Guide Bridge.

5432 cont./
New cylinders.
Gor. 3/7—25/9/20.**G.**
Gor. 11/3—20/5/22.**G.**
Gor. 5/4—5/7/24.**G.**
Gor. 8/5—31/7/26.**G.**
Gor. 14/4—26/5/28.**G.**
Gor. 9/3—13/4/29.**G.**
Gor. 19/7—11/10/30.**G.**
Gor. 14/2/31.**L.**
Frame cracked.
Gor. 28/1—4/3/33.**G.**
Gor. 25/3—29/4/33.**L.**
New cylinders.
Gor. 14—31/12/35.**G.**
Gor. 30/4—28/5/38.**G.**
T.A.B. valves fitted.
Gor. 25/5—8/6/40.**G.**
Gor. 13/3—10/4/43.**G.**
Gor. 10/3—14/4/45.**G.**
Gor. 21/6—26/7/47.**G.**
'AC' Eureka lubrication fitted.
Gor. 9/10—27/11/48.**G.**
New cyls. & T.A.B. valves fitted.
Gor. 27/5—17/6/50.**G.**
Gor. 2—16/12/50.**C/L.**
Gor. 15/11—20/12/52.**H/I.**

BOILERS:
1555.
1560 25/9/20.
1811 5/7/24.
997 31/7/26.
494 13/4/29.
1560 11/10/30.
590 4/3/33.
682 31/12/35.
1675 8/6/40.
598 10/4/43.
3108 14/4/45.
659 26/7/47.
3112 17/6/50.
3112 reno.22002 16/12/50.

SHEDS:
Neasden 3/11/20.
Annesley 2/3/23.
Gorton 10/3/23.
Neasden 5/2/25.
Gorton 28/7/28.
Neasden 10/6/29.
Copley Hill 29/4/33.
Sheffield 28/5/38.
Doncaster 7/1/42.
Darnall 9/8/43.
Trafford Park 1/9/46.
Walton-on-the-Hill 29/12/46.
Darnall 13/4/47.
Brunswick 10/8/47.
Trafford Park 22/5/50.
Northwich 10/2/54.

RENUMBERED:
5432 5/7/24.
2653 9/6/46.

62653 27/11/48.

CONDEMNED: 3/10/55.
Into Gor. for cut up 8/10/55.

5433

WALTER BURGH GAIR

Gorton.

To traffic 10/1913.

REPAIRS:
Gor. 7/8—11/12/20.**G.**
Gor. 20/1—24/3/23.**G.**
Gor. 24/1—18/4/25.**G.**
Gor. 4/9—25/12/26.**G.**
Gor. 13/10—17/11/28.**G.**
Gor. 22/3—26/4/30.**G.**
Gor. 4/7—8/8/31.**G.**
Gor. 26/11—10/12/32.**G.**
Gor. 3—31/3/34.**G.**
Gor. 6/4—11/5/35.**G.**
Gor. 14/3—4/4/36.**G.**
New cylinders.
Gor. 11/12/37—15/1/38.**G.**
Gor. 11/11—30/12/39.**G.**
Gor. 14/11—12/12/42.**G.**
Gor. 21/7—18/8/45.**G.**
Gor. 4—25/10/47.**G.**
Gor. 19/11—10/12/49.**G.**
Gor. 13/1—3/2/51.**H/I.**

BOILERS:
1556.
1554 11/12/20.
1553 25/12/26.
1557 17/11/28.
612 26/4/30.
586 8/8/31.
1813 10/12/32.
724 31/3/34.
683 4/4/36.
659 15/1/38.
682 12/12/42.
3104 18/8/45.
3115 25/10/47.
678 10/12/49.
678 reno.22004 3/2/51.

SHEDS:
Gorton 29/9/22.
Neasden 30/4/25.
Gorton 19/1/29.
Leicester 7/4/32.
Gorton 12/5/32.
Sheffield 25/6/36.
Trafford Park 16/10/49.

RENUMBERED:
433c *"later in 1923".*
5433 at 24/9/24.
2654 15/9/46.

62654 10/12/49.

CONDEMNED: 31/8/53.
Into Gor. for cut up 5/9/53.

5434

THE EARL OF KERRY

Gorton.

To traffic 11/1913.

REPAIRS:
Gor. 16/10/20—12/3/21.**G.**
Gor. 2/6—21/7/23.**G.**
Gor. 22/11/24—17/1/25.**G.**
Gor. 28/8—27/11/26.**G.**
Gor. 5/5—16/6/28.**G.**
To black.
Gor. 6—27/10/28.**L.**
Gor. 24/5—28/6/30.**G.**
New cylinders.
Gor. 12/12/31—9/1/32.**G.**
Gor. 19/8—23/9/33.**G.**
Gor. 25/1—8/2/36.**G.**
Gor. 14/5—23/7/38.**G.**
Gor. 24/8—21/9/40.**G.**
Gor. 3—31/7/43.**G.**
Gor. 25/8—22/9/45.**G.**
Gor. 24/5—5/7/47.**G.**
'AC' Eureka lubrication fitted.
Gor. 7/5—11/6/49.**G.**
Gor. 1—8/10/49.**C/L.**
Gor. 21/4—12/5/51.**H/I.**
Gor. 10/5/52.**C/L.**

BOILERS:
1557.
1555 12/3/21.
1556 21/7/23.
1812 17/1/25.
1554 27/11/26.
988 16/6/28.
612 9/1/32.
673 23/9/33.
590 8/2/36.
3108 23/7/38.
759 21/9/40.
3115 31/7/43.
3116 22/9/45.
759 5/7/47.
3106 11/6/49.
3106 reno. 22008 12/5/51.

SHEDS:
Gorton 8/12/22.
Neasden 28/1/25.
Gorton 24/10/27.
Copley Hill 17/3/33.
Sheffield 23/7/38.
Northwich 10/8/47.

RENUMBERED:
434c 1/9/23.
5434 17/1/25.
2655 27/10/46.
62655 12/3/49.

CONDEMNED: 17/8/53.
Into Gor. for cut up 22/8/53.

5435

SIR CLEMENT ROYDS

Gorton.

To traffic 11/1913.

REPAIRS:
Gor. 26/2—2/4/21.**G.**
Gor. 17/3—26/5/23.**G.**
Gor. 24/1—11/4/25.**G.**
Gor. 4/7/25.**L.**
Gor. 27/11/26—19/2/27.**G.**
Gor. 8/9—10/11/28.**G.**
Gor. 8/3—19/4/30.**G.**
Gor. 4/7—15/8/31.**G.**
Gor. 27/5—24/6/33.**G.**
Gor. 5/1—2/2/35.**G.**
New cylinders.
Gor. 2—16/3/35.**L.**
Main frames fractured.
Gor. 13/2—6/3/37.**G.**
T.A.B. valves fitted.
Gor. 7/1—4/2/39.**G.**
Gor. 28/9—19/10/40.**G.**
Gor. 9/7—15/8/42.**G.**
Gor. 10/6—8/7/44.**G.**
New cylinders.
Gor. 14/4/45.**L.**
Gor. 1/12/45—5/1/46.**G.**
Gor. 8—30/11/46.**L.**
After collision.
Gor. 29/8—6/9/47.**L.**
Gor. 17/4—8/5/48.**G.**
Gor. 5/8—9/9/50.**G.**
Gor. ?/?—18/8/51.**C/L.**
Gor. 8/11—6/12/52.**G.**

BOILERS:
1558.
1556 2/4/21.
1561 26/5/23.
1575 19/4/30.
1554 24/6/33.
649 2/2/35.
3104 6/3/37.
494 4/2/39.
3106 19/10/40.
3102 15/8/42.
678 8/7/44.
3117 8/5/48.
22000 9/9/50.
22023 6/12/52.

During the middle 1930's the steam sanding was changed to gravity applied. It was about the same time before any sight screens were fitted.

About 1934/1935 hinged glass sight screens were fitted on both sides of the cab. Note that cab doors were not fitted. Swindon Shed.

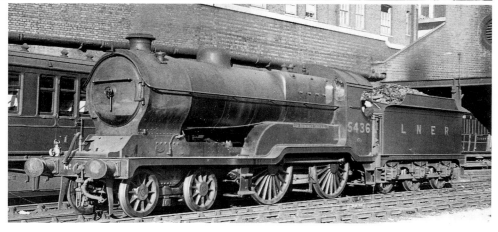

Until about 1946 the smokebox door fastening was by a wheel and a handle (*see* page 95, top) and the top lamp iron was clamped to the handrail. Marylebone.

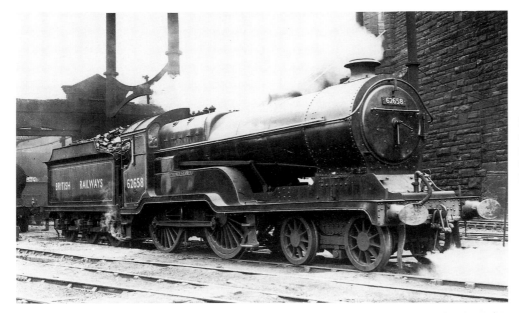

By 1948, the door wheel had been changed to another handle and the top lamp iron was moved down and fixed on to the smokebox door. Brunswick shed.

Throughout, this class had steam brake on engine and tender combined with vacuum for train brakes. The ejector exhaust pipe was always external. The vacuum facility was useful when vacuum operated turntables were introduced.

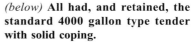

(below) All had, and retained, the standard 4000 gallon type tender with solid coping.

These tenders naturally had water pick-up apparatus, indicated by the spoked handwheel for operating. Exchanges were mostly within the class although similar tenders from two B3 and one B6 class were used. The tender shown was No.6168 coupled to engine 5435 from February 1935 to January 1955. Sheffield Neepsend shed.

As main line express engines they retained their water pick-up gear to withdrawal. This tender was No.437's original.

At Grouping all were in GCR fully lined green livery. Note that the carriage-heating connection at the front end has been removed, probably a 1914-1918 war economy measure.

The first applications of LNER painting on D10 Class were not until May 1923 when Nos.438 (5th), 431 (12th) and 433 (26th) were ex paint shop. They were the only ones to get ampersand and full points and their letters were the $7^{1}/_{2}$in. size. Gorton shed.

Later in 1923, Nos.433 and 438 certainly, and No.431 had the C suffix added. None went into works but all three were at Gorton shed, which was adjoining.

No.435, ex paint shop on 14th July 1923 had LNER, and no suffix unless Gorton shed added one later that year. Use of the suffix began with No.434 (1st September 1923) and others to come out with it were 437 (27th October 1923), 429 (10th November 1923), 436 (1st December 1923) and 430 (12th January 1924).

5435 cont./
SHEDS:
Gorton 28/7/22.
Neasden 26/3/26.
Gorton 3/11/26.
Brunswick ?/3/27.
Gorton 30/10/28.
Sheffield 7/10/31.
Leicester 18/1/32.
Sheffield 28/1/32.
Leicester 7/4/32.
Sheffield 11/5/32.
Neasden 14/4/34.
Sheffield 5/6/34.
Retford 10/9/37.
Sheffield 9/11/37.
Brunswick 5/5/46.
Darnall 14/7/46.
Brunswick 10/8/47.
Trafford Park 23/11/47.
Brunswick 11/9/49.
Trafford Park 22/5/50.
Northwich 26/9/53.

RENUMBERED:
5435 11/4/25.
2656 11/8/46.
62656 8/5/48.

CONDEMNED: 24/1/55.
Into Gor. for cut up 29/1/55.

5436

**SIR BERKELEY SHEF-
FIELD**

Gorton.

To traffic 11/1913.

REPAIRS:
Gor. 20/8—24/12/21.**G**.
Gor. 1/9—24/11/23.**G**.
Gor. 16/5—1/6/25.**G**.
Gor. 30/4—25/8/27.**G**.
Gor. 2/2—23/3/29.**G**.
Gor. 9/5—27/6/31.**G**.
Gor. 29/7—19/8/33.**G**.
Gor. 28/10—25/11/33.**L**.
Gor. 14/12/35—15/2/36.**G**.
New cylinders.
Gor. 28/8—23/10/37.**G**.
Gor. 27/5—24/6/39.**G**.
Gor. 1—30/8/41.**G**.
Gor. 7—23/10/43.**G**.
Gor. 27/10—1/12/45.**G**.
Gor. 24/5—5/7/47.**G**.
New cylinders.
Gor. 18/6—23/7/49.**G**.
Gor. 25/11—16/12/50.**G**.
Gor. 24/5—7/6/52.**C/L**.

BOILERS:
1559.
988 24/12/21.
494 24/11/23.
1554 23/3/29.
673 27/6/31.
338 19/8/33.
614 23/10/37.
3105 24/6/39.
1909 30/8/41.
3114 23/10/43.
3124 1/12/45.
745 5/7/47.
759 23/7/49.
22003 16/12/50.

SHEDS:
Gorton 8/12/22.
Brunswick 17/3/25.
Gorton 6/5/25.
Neasden 8/9/29.
Sheffield 4/7/36.
Northwich 10/8/47.
Darnall 8/9/47.
Brunswick 16/10/49.
Trafford Park 22/5/50.

RENUMBERED:
436c 1/12/23.
5436 1/6/25.
2657 10/11/46.
62657 23/7/49.

CONDEMNED: 16/3/53.
Into Gor. for cut up 21/3/53.

5437

PRINCE GEORGE

Gorton.

To traffic 11/1913.

REPAIRS:
Gor. 6/12/19—31/1/20.**G**.
Gor. 20/8—10/12/21.**G**.
Gor. 30/6—13/10/23.**G**.
Gor. 20/9—8/11/24.**G**.
Gor. 23/1—3/4/26.**G**.
Gor. 25/9—16/10/26.**L**.
Gor. 12/3—5/11/27.**G**.
New frames after casualty.
Gor. 1/6—6/7/29.**G**.
Gor. 7/3—4/4/31.**G**.
Gor. 23/12/33—13/1/34.**G**.
Gor. 18/4—16/5/36.**G**.
Gor. 25/12/37—29/1/38.**G**.
New cylinders.
Gor. 16/12/39—27/1/40.**G**.
Gor. 4—22/5/43.**G**.
Gor. 1—22/7/44.**G**.
New cylinders.

Gor. 26/1—23/2/46.**G**.
Gor. 24/7—7/8/48.**G**.
Gor. 10/6—1/7/50.**G**.
Gor. 27/9—25/10/52.**G**.

BOILERS:
1560.
1553 31/1/20.
1812 13/10/23.
107 8/11/24.
611 3/4/26.
1815 5/11/27.
611 4/4/31.
342 13/1/34.
340 16/5/36.
683 29/1/38.
3108 22/5/43.
3102 22/7/44.
682 23/2/46.
683 7/8/48.
3102 1/7/50.
22022 25/10/52.

SHEDS:
Neasden 13/2/14.
Gorton 10/3/23.
Neasden 23/4/26.
Gorton 2/9/26.
Neasden 2/12/27.
Gorton 1/3/29.
Neasden 1/8/29.
Sheffield 14/4/34.
Neasden 5/6/34.
Annesley 28/1/37.
Sheffield 8/7/38.
Brunswick 10/8/47.
Northwich 17/10/48.
Brunswick 21/11/48.
Trafford Park 22/5/50.
Northwich 8/5/54.

RENUMBERED:
437c 27/10/23.
5437 8/11/24.
2658 20/10/46.
62658 7/8/48.

CONDEMNED: 12/8/55.
Into Gor. for cut up 13/8/55.

5438

WORSLEY-TAYLOR

Gorton.

To traffic 12/1913.

REPAIRS:
Gor. 2/4—18/6/21.**G**.
Gor. 30/12/22—10/3/23.**G**.
Gor. 28/6—4/10/24.**G**.
Gor. 14/8—6/11/26.**G**.

Gor. 4—18/12/26.**L**.
Gor. 17/9—5/11/27.**G**.
Gor. 8/12/28—9/2/29.**G**.
Gor. 8/2—22/3/30.**G**.
Gor. 11/7—29/8/31.**G**.
Gor. 25/2—11/3/33.**G**.
Gor. 14—21/10/33.**L**.
Gor. 17/2—3/3/34.**G**.
Gor. 28/9—19/10/35.**G**.
Gor. 2—23/10/37.**G**.
Gor. 4—25/2/39.**G**.
Gor. 17/5—28/6/41.**G**.
Gor. 18/5—6/6/42.**H**.
New cylinders.
Gor. 10—26/2/44.**G**.
Gor. 22/12/45—19/1/46.**G**.
New cylinders.
Gor. 18/10/47—24/1/48.**G**.
Gor. 17/12/49—21/1/50.**G**.
Gor. 1/12/51—26/1/52.**G**.

BOILERS:
1561.
107 18/6/21.
1671 4/10/24.
107 6/11/26.
1811 29/8/31.
987 11/3/33.
611 3/3/34.
759 19/10/35.
163 23/10/37.
3104 25/2/39.
745 26/2/44.
3107 19/1/46.
3108 24/1/48.
3107 21/1/50.
22013 26/1/52.

SHEDS:
Gorton 8/12/22.
Sheffield 17/6/36.
Retford 29/1/37.
Sheffield 10/9/37.
Retford 9/11/37.
Sheffield 28/6/39.
Doncaster 31/12/41.
Langwith Jct. 15/2/43.
Darnall 29/8/43.
Brunswick 16/10/49.
Trafford Park 22/5/50.
Northwich 21/3/53.

RENUMBERED:
438c *"later in 1923".*
5438 4/10/24.
2659 20/10/46.
ᴇ2659 24/1/48.
62659 21/1/50.

CONDEMNED: 22/11/54.
Into Gor. for cut up 27/11/54.

(above) No.432 retained GC livery until it went to works on 5th April 1924 and, ex paint shop 12th July, it was No.5432 in standard LNER green livery. All the others then took this style until June 1928 when black was prescribed for this class.

The first five engines into black with single red lining retained number on tender. They were: 5435 (10th Nov.), 5433 (17th Nov.), 5430 (15th Dec.) in 1928, 5438 (9th Feb.) and 5436 (23rd Mar.), 1929.

The number was moved to the cab from March 1929 and tender letters became 12in. in place of 7°in. hitherto. This style continued until war economies had to be made.

From November 1941 the red lining was dropped and from July 1942 until January 1946 only NE was put on the tender. Darnall shed.

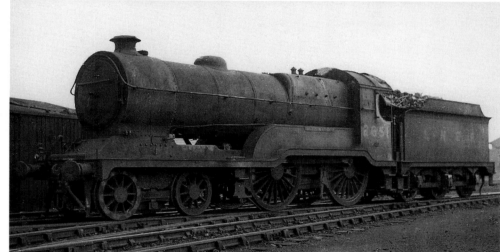

From January 1946 LNER was restored but still on unlined black. During that year renumbering as 2650 to 2659 took place between June and November.

After Nationalisation two got BRITISH RAILWAYS on the tender and the regional prefix E to their number. They were E2659 (24th January 1948) and E2652 (31st January 1948). The first with full BR number was 62656, ex works on 8th May 1948 still unlined, and with 12in. painted figures including the modified 6, and with only 8in. lettering on the tender. No smokebox number plate was then fitted as they were only introduced in June 1948.

No.62658, out on 7th August 1948, was a special case because it got full red, cream and grey lining for display at Chesterfield to mark the centenary of George Stephenson's death. Numbers and letters at 10in. now matched, but modified 6 was used on cab and on the smokebox number plate.

Unlined black continued but from 27th November 1948 on 62653 the correct Gill sans 6 appeared on the cab. Smokebox plates still had modified 6 and 62651, 62652, 62653, 62655, 62657 were so cast.

The change to the large version of the BR emblem began on 62650 (24th September 1949) followed by 62654 (10th December 1949) and 62659 (21st January 1950) but 62656 did not get it until 9th September 1950. Only these four had the correct 6 and 9 on their smokebox plates. Brunswick shed.

Belated recognition was accorded the last three to get heavy repairs in 1952 as they joined 62658 in being fully lined out. They were 62652 (13th September), 62656 (6th December) and 62653 (20th December). The other six were still in unlined black to withdrawal. Manchester (Central) station locomotive servicing yard.

Two more engines, Nos.501 and 502, were built at Gorton during September and October 1922 to the same design, and painting, as the previous batch. No.502 did not however leave the paint shop until the 6th January 1923.

(left) Four further engines, Nos.503, 504, 505 and 511, were ex works between the 4th November and 23rd December 1922 and thus counted as Great Central Railway stock. However, they were not ex paint shop until after Grouping and their new LNER ownership was indicated. Dates to traffic in 1923 were: 503 (27th January), 504 (3rd March), 505 (27th January) and 511 (14th April). Neasden shed.

(below) Superheater elements were originally protected from burning by Robinson's combined blower and steam circulating valve with a header discharge valve on the side of the smokebox. This system was still used by No.5502 to April 1926. Neasden shed, June 1925.

CLASS D 11/1

5506

BUTLER-HENDERSON

Gorton.

To traffic 12/1919.

REPAIRS:
Gor. 21/1—20/5/22.**G.**
Gor. 22/3—7/6/24.**G.**
Gor. 1/8—14/11/25.**G.**
Gor. 6/3/26.**L.**
Gor. 5/2—23/4/27.**G.**
Gor. 1/12/28—19/1/29.**G.**
Gor. 22/11—27/12/30.**G.**
Gor. 17/9—15/10/32.**G.**
Gor. 27/5—8/7/33.**G.**
Gor. 28/4—12/5/34.**G.**
Gor. 21/3—16/5/36.**G.**
Gor. 30/4—21/5/38.**G.**
Gor. 20/1—10/2/40.**G.**
Gor. 18/2—6/3/43.**G.**
Gor. 8—29/9/45.**G.**
Gor. 6/12/47—10/1/48.**G.**
Gor. 10/9—1/10/49.**G.**
Gor. 15/12/51—19/1/52.**G.**
Gor. 11/7/53.**C/L.**
Tender tank only.
Gor. 13/11—25/12/54.**H/I.**
Gor. 9/6—28/7/56.**C/L.**
Gor. 5—12/1/57.**C/L.**
Gor. 6/7—17/8/57.**G.**
Gor. 29/10/60.*Not repaired.*

BOILERS:
1811.
1814 7/6/24.
1575 14/11/25.
1555 23/4/27.
611 19/1/29.
338 27/12/30.
668 8/7/33.
1671 12/5/34.
670 16/5/36.
3107 21/5/38.
598 10/2/40.
3117 6/3/43.
614 29/9/45.
3107 10/1/48.
3116 1/10/49.
22015 19/1/52.
22001 17/8/57.

SHEDS:
Neasden 13/3/20.
Gorton 2/6/25.

Copley Hill 2/7/27.
Gorton 29/11/28.
Copley Hill 27/2/29.
Gorton 14/10/30.
Copley Hill 6/3/31.
Neasden 29/8/32.
Sheffield 9/8/38.
Mexborough 10/8/43.
Neasden 8/2/46.
Immingham 14/7/47.
Trafford Park 12/3/51.
Lincoln 25/10/53.
Darnall 24/3/57.

RENUMBERED:
5506 7/6/24.
2660 19/10/46.
62660 1/10/49.

WITHDRAWN: 5/11/60.
Restored for preservation.

5507

**GERARD POWYS
DEWHURST**

Gorton.

To traffic 2/1920.

REPAIRS:
Gor. 24/9—19/11/21.**G.**
Gor. 23/6—11/8/23.**G.**
Gor. 2/2—1/3/24.**L.**
Gor. 25/10/24—17/1/25.**G.**
Gor. 17/7—25/9/26.**G.**
Gor. 11/8—6/10/28.**G.**
Gor. 22/2—19/4/30.**G.**
Gor. 21/5—11/6/32.**G.**
Gor. 23/9—14/10/33.**G.**
Gor. 24/11—15/12/34.**G.**
Gor. 13/6—18/7/36.**G.**
Gor. 25/6—16/7/38.**G.**
Gor. 18/1—15/2/41.**G.**
Gor. 21/10—13/11/43.**G.**
Gor. 3—17/6/44.**L.**
*New type cylinders and long
travel valves fitted.*
Gor. 17—24/3/45.**L.**
Gor. 29/6—31/8/46.**G.**
Gor. 4—31/12/48.**G.**
Gor. 17/2—10/3/51.**G.**
Gor. 30/1—20/2/54.**G.**
Gor. 28/4—2/6/56.**G.**
Gor. 17/10—16/11/59.**C/L.**

BOILERS:
1812.
1555 11/8/23.
1552 25/9/26.
1890 11/6/32.
612 14/10/33.
107 15/12/34.
745 18/7/36.
670 16/7/38.
586 15/2/41.
3118 13/11/43.
3113 31/12/48.
22005 10/3/51.
22004 20/2/54.
22017 2/6/56.

SHEDS:
Neasden 14/5/20.
Gorton 15/3/24.
Copley Hill 1/4/27.
Neasden 9/5/32.
Gorton 19/9/35.
Neasden 18/11/35.
Immingham 14/7/47.
Trafford Park 24/3/51.
Northwich 12/3/55.
Darnall 27/4/58.
Staveley 7/6/59.

RENUMBERED:
507c 15/9/23.
5507 1/3/24.
2661 21/10/46.
62661 31/12/48.

CONDEMNED: 18/11/60.
Into Don. for cut up 18/11/60.

5508

PRINCE OF WALES

Gorton.

To traffic 3/1920.

REPAIRS:
Gor. 21/1—8/4/22.**G.**
Gor. 16/2—19/4/24.**G.**
Gor. 26/9—28/11/25.**G.**
Gor. 7/5—30/6/27.**G.**
Gor. 6/10—10/11/28.**G.**
Gor. 14/6—26/7/30.**G.**
Gor. 14/7—1/8/31.**G.**
Gor. 10/12/32—21/1/33.**G.**
Gor. 26/5—23/6/34.**G.**

Gor. 28/9—7/12/35.**G.**
Gor. 13/3—3/4/37.**G.**
Gor. 3—24/12/38.**G.**
Gor. 15/2—8/3/41.**G.**
Gor. 24/2—13/3/43.**G.**
Gor. 2—23/12/44.**G.**
Gor. 19/5/45.**L.**
Boiler backplate weld.
Gor. 29/9—6/10/45.**L.**
Gor. 3/5—7/6/47.**G.**
Gor. 23/4—21/5/49.**G.**
New cyls & long travel valves.
Gor. 22/7—26/8/50.**G.**
Gor. 22/11—27/12/52.**G.**
Gor. 30/10—30/11/54.**N/C.**
Gor. 6/8—17/9/55.**G.**
Gor. 17/8—14/9/57.**G.**

BOILERS:
1814.
670 19/4/24.
1560 28/11/25.
331 30/6/27.
1811 10/11/28.
260 1/8/31.
586 21/1/33.
668 23/6/34.
611 7/12/35.
494 3/4/37.
3111 24/12/38.
605 8/3/41.
659 13/3/43.
605 23/12/44.
3101 7/6/47.
3125 21/5/49.
707 26/8/50.
22024 27/12/52.
22019 17/9/55.
22018 14/9/57.

SHEDS:
Neasden 24/5/20.
Gorton 28/1/25.
Sheffield 3/4/37.
Retford 8/7/39.
Lincoln 19/7/39.
Immingham 25/1/40.
Trafford Park 22/10/50.
Northwich 1/10/55.
Newton Heath 12/5/56.
Northwich 19/5/56.
Darnall 27/4/58.

RENUMBERED:
5508 19/4/24.
2662 13/10/46.
62662 21/5/49.

WORKS CODES:- Bpk - Beyer, Peacock. Dar- Darlington. Don - Doncaster. Ghd - Gateshead. Gor - Gorton. Str - Stratford. Wfd - Woodford shed.
REPAIR CODES:- **C/H** - Casual Heavy. **C/L** - Casual Light. **G** - General. **H**- Heavy. **H/I** - Heavy Intermediate. **L** - Light. **L/I** - Light Intermediate. **N/C** - Non-Classified.

99

5508 cont./
CONDEMNED: 8/8/60.
Into Don. for cut up 8/8/60.

5509

PRINCE ALBERT

Gorton.

To traffic 3/1920.

REPAIRS:
Gor. 11/2—6/5/22.**G.**
Gor. 21/6—16/8/24.**G.**
Gor. 1/8—31/10/25.**G.**
Gor. 9/4—4/6/27.**G.**
Gor. 7/4—2/6/28.**G.**
Gor. 6/4—4/5/29.**G.**
Gor. 27/9—1/11/30.**G.**
Gor. 12—31/12/31.**G.**
Gor. 31/12/32—28/1/33.**G.**
Gor. 2—30/12/33.**G.**
Gor. 23/2—6/4/35.**G.**
Gor. 4/4—2/5/36.**G.**
Gor. 27/11—18/12/37.**G.**
Gor. 1/4—6/5/39.**L.**
Gor. 8/6—13/7/40.**G.**
Gor. 21/12/40—11/1/41.**L.**
After collision.
Gor. 19/9—17/10/42.**G.**
Gor. 6—11/9/43.**L.**
Gor. 6—27/5/44.**G.**
Gor. 13/10—8/12/45.**G.**
New cylinders and long travel valves fitted.
Gor. 29/3—3/5/47.**G.**
Gor. 11/6—13/8/49.**G.**
Gor. 20/5—3/6/50.**C/L.**
Tender changed.
Gor. 26/5—16/6/51.**G.**
Gor. 31/5—14/6/52.**C/L.**
Gor. 24/4—29/5/54.**G.**
Gor. 16/6—6/10/56.**G.**

BOILERS:
1815.
1560 16/8/24.
668 31/10/25.
331 4/5/29.
668 1/11/30.
1578 31/12/31.
260 28/1/33.
670 30/12/33.
659 2/5/36.
759 18/12/37.
682 13/7/40.
3106 17/10/42.
612 27/5/44.
586 3/5/47.
645 13/8/49.
22010 16/6/51.
22005 29/5/54.
22026 6/10/56.

SHEDS:
Neasden 8/4/20.
Gorton 6/2/25.
Neasden 10/1/31.
Gorton 15/1/31.
Sheffield 26/6/33.
Gorton 19/2/35.
Sheffield 19/11/38.
Immingham 11/9/43.
Trafford Park 12/3/50.
Heaton Mersey 22/5/50.
Lincoln 21/7/54.
Doncaster 22/8/54.
Lincoln 29/8/54.
Darnall 24/3/57.
Staveley 13/4/58.

RENUMBERED:
5509 16/8/24.
2663 13/10/46.
62663 13/8/49.

CONDEMNED: 23/5/60.
Cut up at Stratford.

5510

PRINCESS MARY

Gorton.

To traffic 5/1920.

REPAIRS:
Gor. 3/9—3/12/21.**G.**
Gor. 29/9—1/12/23.**G.**
Gor. 13/6—22/8/25.**G.**
Gor. 10/10/25.**L.**
Indicating gear fitted.
Gor. 30/4—18/6/27.**G.**
Gor. 22/9—27/10/28.**G.**
Gor. 15/2—15/3/30.**G.**
Gor. 4/4—9/5/31.**G.**
Gor. 11/3—1/4/33.**G.**
Gor. 2/9/33.**L.**
Gor. 7/7—18/8/34.**G.**
Gor. 2/5—4/7/36.**G.**
Gor. 26/11—10/12/38.**G.**
Gor. 6/11—6/12/41.**G.**
Gor. 17/3—8/4/44.**G.**
Gor. 11/8—15/9/45.**G.**
New cylinders and long travel valves fitted.
Str. 12/9—12/10/46.**L.**
Gor. 7/2—3/4/48.**G.**
Gor. 15—29/4/50.**G.**
Gor. 28/7—18/8/51.**H/I.**
Gor. 6—20/9/52.**C/H.**
Gor. 2—30/1/54.**G.**
Gor. 30/7—13/8/55.**C/L.**
Gor. 24/3—28/4/56.**G.**
Gor. 9/11—14/12/57.**C/L.**

BOILERS:
1890.
260 1/12/23.
1671 27/10/28.
977 9/5/31.
1578 1/4/33.
586 18/8/34.
745 10/12/38.
612 6/12/41.
3116 8/4/44.
3122 15/9/45.
724 3/4/48.
3128 29/4/50.
3128 reno.22011 18/8/51.
22009 30/1/54.
22006 28/4/56.

SHEDS:
Neasden 17/9/20.
Gorton 15/3/24.
Copley Hill 29/11/28.
Gorton 27/2/29.
Copley Hill 19/6/31.
Neasden 8/2/33.
Immingham 14/7/47.
Trafford Park 23/1/51.
Northwich 12/3/55.
Newton Heath 5/5/56.
Northwich 19/5/56.
Darnall 27/4/58.

RENUMBERED:
510c 22/12/23.
5510 22/8/25.
2664 23/9/46.
62664 3/4/48.

CONDEMNED: 8/8/60.
Into Don. for cut up 8/8/60.

5501

MONS

Gorton.

To traffic 9/1922.

REPAIRS:
Gor. 30/8—1/11/24.**G.**
Gor. 20/3—5/6/26.**G.**
Gor. 21/1—10/3/28.**G.**
Gor. 21—28/7/28.**L.**
Gor. 15/2—15/3/30.**G.**
Gor. 27/6—1/8/31.**G.**
Gor. 25/3—22/4/33.**G.**
Gor. 20/10—3/11/34.**G.**
Gor. 9/11—28/12/35.**G.**
Gor. 31/12/36—30/1/37.**G.**
Gor. 2—30/7/38.**G.**
Gor. 19/8—30/9/39.**G.**
Gor. 24/10—15/11/41.**G.**
Gor. 16/11—4/12/43.**G.**
Gor. 30/3—4/5/46.**G.**

Gor. 15/5—12/6/48.**G.**
Gor. 29/10—19/11/49.**G.**
Gor. 7—21/10/50.**C/L.**
Gor. 10/11/51—2/2/52.**G.**
New cyls & long travel valves.
Gor. 11/12/54—29/1/55.**L/I.**

BOILERS:
331.
1815 1/11/24.
1576 5/6/26.
260 15/3/30.
1554 1/8/31.
1674 3/11/34.
678 28/12/35.
612 30/1/37.
657 15/11/41.
586 4/12/43.
593 4/5/46.
678 12/6/48.
3127 19/11/49.
22012 2/2/52.

SHEDS:
Neasden 30/9/22.
Copley Hill 11/4/28.
Gorton 22/6/31.
Sheffield 7/6/33.
Gorton 22/2/35.
Sheffield 1/6/37.
Langwith Jct. 29/8/43.
Lincoln 21/7/44.
Mexborough 1/10/44.
Immingham 14/7/47.
Trafford Park 26/3/50.
Heaton Mersey 22/5/50.
Northwich 4/12/54.
Darnall 27/4/58.

RENUMBERED:
5501 1/11/24.
2665 4/5/46.
62665 12/6/48.

CONDEMNED: 8/5/59.
Into Gor. for cut up 9/5/59.

5502

ZEEBRUGGE

Gorton.

To traffic 10/1922.

REPAIRS:
Gor. 20/9—22/11/24.**G.**
Gor. 10/4—26/6/26.**G.**
Gor. 17/12/27—21/1/28.**G.**
Gor. 16/2—6/4/29.**G.**
Gor. 5/7—16/8/30.**G.**
Gor. 4—25/6/32.**G.**
Gor. 5—19/8/33.**G.**

For its next spell of work between shopping, from June 1926 to December 1927, No.5502 had to manage without element protection. A Gresley type header could not be used in conjunction with the large base diameter of the original chimney. Marylebone.

In March 1924, No.5507 had its chimney changed to an experimental type, and this allowed a single Gresley anti-vacuum valve to be fitted in the central position. It is believed this was a trial in connection with the design of the Part 2 engines.

In late 1925 the introduction of the 'plant pot' chimney allowed the use of a superheater header using the Gresley anti-vacuum valve and (apart from 5503 and 5507) there was one at each end of the header. Note evidence of the recent removal of the Robinson type of header discharge valve. Grantham.

The other side of No.5506 showing the anti-vacuum valve on that side also. These were retained to November 1930, despite a change of chimney to the 'plant pot' type which permitted the central position anti-vacuum valve. Doncaster, September 1930.

In January 1928, No.5502 was fitted with 'plant pot' chimney and also a central anti-vacuum valve and all duly got a valve of this type and position.

(above) Although the 'plant pot' chimney reduced height from rail to 12ft 10⅞in. from 13ft 1⅞in., the cab and dome heights were not altered so this Part remained outside the composite loading gauge. Gorton shed.

(left) About 1933, another change of chimney type began with the introduction of a design very similar to the original but giving the same height as the 'plant pot'. All duly got this style, irrespective of dome height.

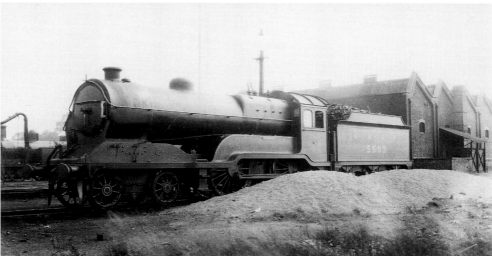

(above) The Part 2 engines (see later volume) perforce had to have reduced dome height to work in Scotland, so to permit exchange of boilers, all the boilers for the D10 and D11 classes built from 1924 had a short dome. This brought the chimney and dome under 13ft 0in. but the cab roof remained above that height. Swindon, March 1934.

(right) The cast chimney put on No.5507 for trial was supplemented by a similar but taller chimney carried by No.5503 in 1926-1928. This was the only one of this type to be fitted, and it was discarded when taken off 5503.

After the changes in the 1930's, there was only a minor one later. In the 1950's, Nos.62663, 62667 and 62668 acquired dome covers with a flattened top. Derby ex-LMS shed.

(above) **All had the whistle mounted on the firebox in front of the cab, and although its top was the highest point above rail level, no dimension for it was ever included on the Diagram.**

(left) **The first five engines did not have an ash ejector when built but it was fitted to them during 1921 and 1922. Steam for the ash ejector entered the rear of the smokebox until 1925. The 1922 engines came out with ash ejector fitted and they too had the short pipe (*see* page 109, bottom). However, the scoring of the front tube plate led to the steam supply point being moved forward and a longer pipe being put on (*see* opposite, top). Nottingham (Victoria).**

Around 1945/46, the ash ejector was removed from the whole of the class.

(above) On the original boilers, washout facilities were provided by two hand holes and five large plugs on the right hand side of the firebox. Note the longer steam supply pipe for the ash ejector. Gorton shed.

(right) On the replacement boilers the positions were the same but the plugs were smaller.

Small plugs were also fitted on the left-hand side where there were four but there were three hand holes on the shoulder.

Until 1937 the piston valves were 10in. diameter and had a maximum travel of 4¼in. The reversing arm was straight and the cylinder fixing bolts were in a single line curved up at the ends. Marylebone station.

In January 1937, No.5505 was fitted with new cylinders on which the valves were 8in. diameter with a maximum travel of 5¾in. The cylinders now had two parallel rows of fixing bolts and the reversing arm had a noticeable curve. Charwelton, July 1937.

5502 cont./
Gor. 2—16/2/35.**G.**
Gor. 21/3—25/4/36.**G.**
Gor. 13—27/3/37.**L.**
Gor. 1/1—5/2/38.**G.**
Gor. 8/7—5/8/39.**L.**
Frame cracked.
Gor. 7—28/9/40.**G.**
Gor. 16/4—1/5/43.**G.**
Gor. 14—28/10/44.**G.**
Gor. 7/6—2/8/47.**G.**
New cyls & long travel valves.
Gor. 27/8—24/9/49.**G.**
Gor. 14—28/6/52.**G.**
Gor. 28/3—11/4/53.**C/L.**
After collision.
Gor. 6/11—18/12/54.**G.**
Gor. 2—30/3/57.**G.**

BOILERS:
  334.
    673 22/11/24.
  1560 21/1/28.
  1576 16/8/30.
    683 25/6/32.
    598 19/8/33.
    659 16/2/35.
    724 25/4/36.
  3106 5/2/38.
  3108 28/9/40.
    605 1/5/43.
  3106 28/10/44.
  3124 2/8/47.
  3101 24/9/49.
 22020 28/6/52.
 22001 18/12/54.
 22004 30/3/57.

SHEDS:
Neasden 21/10/22.
Copley Hill 23/1/30.
Gorton 9/5/30.
Copley Hill 14/10/30.
Gorton 6/3/31.
Sheffield 14/11/33.
Gorton 16/2/35.
Sheffield 13/2/39.
Mexborough 10/8/43.
Immingham 10/8/47.
Trafford Park 22/10/50.
Immingham 8/2/53.
Mexborough 21/6/53.
Lincoln 27/9/53.
Darnall 31/3/57.

RENUMBERED:
 5502 22/11/24.
 2666 21/7/46.
62666 24/9/49.

CONDEMNED: 5/12/60.
Into Don. for cut up 5/12/60.

5503

SOMME

Gorton.

To traffic 4/11/1922. *Put into traffic as L. & N. E. R. 27/1/23.*

REPAIRS:
Gor. 18/10—13/12/24.**G.**
Gor. 17/7—16/10/26.**G.**
Gor. 24/3—12/5/28.**G.**
Gor. 6/7—10/8/29.**G.**
Gor. 25/10—29/11/30.**G.**
Gor. 31/12/31—23/1/32.**G.**
Gor. 15/4—20/5/33.**G.**
Gor. 17/3—14/4/34.**G.**
New cylinders.
Gor. 24/8—21/9/35.**G.**
Gor. 31/12/36—30/1/37.**G.**
Gor. 13/11/37—15/1/38.**H.**
Frame cracked.
Gor. 15/6—6/7/40.**G.**
Gor. 28/9—5/10/40.**L.**
Gor. 19—26/10/40.**L.**
Gor. 11/9—2/10/43.**G.**
Gor. 15/9—27/10/45.**G.**
New cyls & long travel valves.
Gor. 17/5—14/6/47.**G.**
New cylinders.
Gor. 1—22/10/49.**G.**
Gor. 23/2—15/3/52.**G.**
Gor. 16/10—27/11/54.**G.**
Gor. 3/11—1/12/56.**G.**

BOILERS:
  338.
    334 13/12/24.
    670 16/10/26.
  1577 10/8/29.
    331 29/11/30.
    668 23/1/32.
    977 20/5/33.
    759 14/4/34.
    494 21/9/35.
     60 30/1/37.
  3114 6/7/40.
  3113 2/10/43.
  3117 27/10/45.
  3102 14/6/47.
  3121 22/10/49.
 22017 15/3/52.
 22010 27/11/54.
 22016 1/12/56.

SHEDS:
Neasden 4/11/22.
Gorton 20/7/28.
Copley Hill 25/7/28.
Gorton 11/8/28.
Heaton Mersey 11/9/39.
Gorton 24/9/39.
Heaton Mersey 7/5/42.
Sheffield 7/6/42.

Langwith Jct. 20/6/42.
Lincoln 17/8/44.
Mexborough 1/10/44.
Immingham 14/7/47.
Trafford Park 27/1/51.
Immingham 8/2/53.
Boston 15/3/53.
Mexborough 21/6/53.
Lincoln 27/9/53.
Darnall 24/3/57.

RENUMBERED:
 5503 13/12/24.
 2667 21/7/46.
62667 22/10/49.

CONDEMNED: 12/8/60.
Into Don. for cut up 12/8/60.

5504

JUTLAND

Gorton.

To traffic 18/11/1922. *Put into traffic as L. & N. E. R. 3/3/23.*

REPAIRS:
Gor. 1/11—20/12/24.**G.**
Gor. 3/4—30/6/26.**G.**
Gor. 11/2—24/3/28.**G.**
Gor. 24/8—28/9/29.**G.**
Gor. 22/11—27/12/30.**G.**
Gor. 23/4—21/5/32.**G.**
Gor. 7/10—4/11/33.**G.**
Gor. 2—16/2/35.**G.**
Gor. 4—25/7/36.**G.**
Gor. 5/11—17/12/38.**G.**
Gor. 27/4—23/5/42.**G.**
Gor. 2—25/9/43.**G.**
Gor. 2—23/2/46.**G.**
Gor. 19/10—9/11/46.**H.**
New cyls & long travel valves.
Gor. 1—15/5/48.**G.**
Gor. 6/5—3/6/50.**G.**
Gor. 24/5—14/6/52.**L/I.**
Gor. 26/3—14/5/55.**G.**
Gor. 6/9/58.**C/L.**
Tender repaired.

BOILERS:
  339.
    340 20/12/24.
  1577 30/6/26.
    673 24/3/28.
    670 28/9/29.
  1577 27/12/30.
    342 21/5/32.
  1890 4/11/33.
    657 16/2/35.
  3102 25/7/36.
    614 23/5/42.
    593 25/9/43.

3113 23/2/46.
  707 15/5/48.
  724 3/6/50.
  724 reno.22019 14/6/52.
22020 14/5/55.

SHEDS:
Neasden 18/11/22.
Gorton 10/7/26.
Neasden 2/9/26.
Immingham 14/7/47.
Trafford Park 26/11/50.
Darnall 27/4/58.

RENUMBERED:
 5504 20/12/24.
 2668 19/10/46.
62668 15/5/48.

CONDEMNED: 17/11/60.
Into Don. for cut up 17/11/60.

5505

YPRES

Gorton.

To traffic 9/12/1922. *Put into traffic as L. & N. E. R. 27/1/23.*

REPAIRS:
Gor. 20/9—15/11/24.**G.**
Gor. 19/6—28/8/26.**G.**
Gor. 31/3—19/5/28.**G.**
Gor. 3/8—14/9/29.**G.**
Gor. 27/12/30—24/1/31.**G.**
Gor. 17/9—8/10/32.**G.**
Gor. 10/2—3/3/34.**G.**
Gor. 9/2—9/3/35.**G.**
Gor. 21/11/36—30/1/37.**G.**
New cyls & long travel valves.
Gor. 23/12/39—13/1/40.**G.**
Gor. 11/6—3/7/43.**G.**
Gor. 14/10—6/11/43.**L.**
After collision.
Gor. 30/6—11/8/45.**G.**
Gor. 29/11—27/12/47.**G.**
Gor. 12—26/2/49.**L.**
Gor. 19/11—17/12/49.**G.**
Gor. 5/4—3/5/52.**G.**
Gor. 28/8—25/9/54.**H/I.**
Gor. 26/1—23/2/57.**G.**

BOILERS:
  340.
    331 15/11/24.
    340 28/8/26.
  1812 19/5/28.
  1813 24/1/31.
  1576 8/10/32.
    707 3/3/34.
    598 9/3/35.
    593 13/1/40.

5505 cont./
1675 3/7/43.
724 11/8/45.
3112 27/12/47.
3114 17/12/49.
22018 3/5/52.
22005 23/2/57.

SHEDS:
Neasden 9/12/22.
Immingham 14/7/47.
Trafford Park 26/11/50.
Northwich 24/4/52.
Darnall 4/5/58.

RENUMBERED:
5505 15/11/24.
2669 12/10/46.
62669 26/2/49.

CONDEMNED: 12/8/60.
Into Don. for cut up 12/8/60.

_____

(below) **From June 1944, Gorton put the longer travel valves on to Part 1 engines, and when 62665 was so altered only 62660 remained with the original type valves, and these it retained to withdrawal. Darnall shed, September 1958.**

5511

MARNE

Gorton.

To traffic 23/12/1922. *Put into traffic as L. & N. E. R. 14/4/23.*

REPAIRS:
Gor. 13/12/24—28/2/25.**G**.
Don. 16—30/5/25.**L**.
Gor. 7/8—30/10/26.**G**.
Gor. 25/2—7/4/28.**G**.
Gor. 11/5—15/6/29.**G**.
Gor. 27/9—8/11/30.**G**.
Gor. 14/11—5/12/31.**G**.
Gor. 11/3—8/4/33.**G**.
Gor. 15/12/34—5/1/35.**G**.
Gor. 16/5—6/6/36.**G**.
Gor. 18/9—6/11/37.**G**.
Gor. 8—22/6/40.**G**.
Gor. 21/2—7/3/42.**G**.
Gor. 11—29/1/44.**G**.
Gor. 31/3—5/5/45.**G**.
New cyls & long travel valves.
Gor. 4/1—1/2/47.**G**.
Gor. 19/3—23/4/49.**G**.
Gor. 24/2—17/3/51.**G**.
Gor. 5—23/5/53.**C/L**.
Gor. 23/10—4/12/54.**G**.
Gor. 19/1—16/2/57.**G**.

BOILERS:
342.
1577 7/4/28.
342 15/6/29.
107 5/12/31.
593 8/4/33.
612 5/1/35.
339 6/6/36.
611 6/11/37.
678 22/6/40.
745 7/3/42.
3121 29/1/44.
659 5/5/45.
3125 1/2/47.
3118 23/4/49.
22006 17/3/51.
22011 4/12/54.
22010 16/2/57.

SHEDS:
Neasden 23/12/22.
Gorton 7/3/25.
Copley Hill 14/2/27.
Neasden 16/4/28.
Gorton 19/7/29.
Sheffield 18/5/33.
Gorton 12/2/34.
Sheffield 21/11/38.
Gorton 7/1/39.
Sheffield 7/6/42.
Langwith Jct. 15/6/42.
Immingham 29/10/44.
Walton-on-the-Hill 31/3/50.

Trafford Park 22/5/50.
Immingham 25/10/53.
Lincoln 6/5/56.
Darnall 24/3/57.

RENUMBERED:
5511 28/2/25.
2670 13/10/46.
62670 23/4/49.

CONDEMNED: 15/11/60.
Into Don. for cut up 15/11/60.

_____

(above) **Until about 1932/1933, the cab sides were not fitted with hinged screens to help forward vision. Sanding was applied by steam ahead of the leading coupled wheels and for running in reverse it was applied by gravity from boxes at the front of the tender.**

(right) **Around 1933-1935, hinged glass sightscreens were fitted to the cab on both sides. About the same time, the forward sanding was changed from steam to gravity application.**

Somewhat surprisingly on top line express passenger engines, a carriage heater connection at the front end was provided from the start. Guide Bridge.

All eleven D11's had a wheel and a handle for smokebox door fastening and the top lamp iron was clamped to the handrail. Nottingham (Victoria).

Only during 1945/1946 were changes made. The wheel was then replaced by a second handle, and on most, the top lamp iron was moved down onto the smokebox door. At its May 1946 general repair the lamp iron move was missed on 2665 and it remained on the handrail to May 1948.

All did have the iron moved on to the door, to a position (*see* page 117, bottom) which proved too low when smokebox number plates were put on, and it had then to be fixed higher. Derby ex-LMS shed, October 1953.

Great Central type buffers with parallel shank and oval head were the normal equipment. In later years the width across the heads tended to diminish but most kept this type to withdrawal.

No.62665 was the only one noted as changed to the Group Standard type buffer shanks which (unusually) housed GC type oval heads. The change was made in February 1952. Heaton Mersey shed, June 1952.

(below) This buffer variation was not applied to tenders as that with 62666 had the normal GS type. Darnall shed, June 1958.

(above) **The standard tender throughout was the 4000-gallon type and water pick-up gear was retained. Those built for the 1922 engines were self-trimming type and had a wider body with less flare to the coping than on the five built for Nos.506, 507, 508, 509 and 510.**

(left) **No.5509 kept its original tender to December 1931. Note the standard plain cover plates to the axleboxes.**

After Grouping, when B3 class Nos.6164, 6165, 6166, 6167, 6168 and 6169 were sent to work on the GN mainline they were given the more modern self-trimming tenders from the 1922 built D11 class. The latter then took the B3 tenders. These had been fitted with Iracier axleboxes which were recognisable by their shield shape covers, but some of which were already being replaced by standard type.

The first five, and Nos.501 and 502 of the 1922 engines, were painted in GCR passenger livery. No.501 remained in GC livery until it went for repair on 30th August 1924 and No.502 likewise until 20th September 1924.

Ex paint shop on 27th January 1923, new engines 503 and 505 were in GC green and lining with the crest on the splasher but with 6in. L.&N.E.R. over the 12in. number on the tender. No.503 went to York to take part in the inspection by Directors on 31st January 1923 to choose Group liveries and No.505 was done as reserve. No.504, out on 3rd March 1923, was in the same style except for having the Company's initials in 7$\frac{1}{2}$in. letters. Marylebone.

(above) The last of the class did not leave the paint shop until 14th April 1923 and it differed in not having a lining panel on the cab side and no GC crest on the splasher. The green is believed to have been the GC shade, not the lighter LNER green. Neasden shed, July 1923.

None of the first five got either ampersand or full points, but 507 (15th September 1923) and 510 (22nd December 1923) had the C suffix to their tender numbering. Nottingham (Victoria).

No.5507 out from a light repair on 1st March 1924 was the first to get the 1924 Group numbering and it also got 5507 on the large GC style brass plates on the cab. Nos.5508 (19th April 1924) and 5506 (7th June 1924) also got these large cab side plates. Nottingham (Victoria).

No.5509, out on 16th August 1924, did not get the large brass plates and the Group Standard type was applied thenceforward. The green lined livery was continued to the June 1928 economies.

The first four into black livery retained their number on the tender. These were 5507 (6th October), 5510 (27th October), 5508 (10th November), in 1928, and 5506 (19th January 1929). Grantham.

From March 1929, the number was put on the cab side and the LNER became 12in. letters. Single red lining was put on until November 1941.

From July 1942 to January 1946 only NE was used on the tender and the unlined black was continued. Cleethorpes, May 1946.

LNER on the tender was resumed from January 1946 and this tender was so lettered on 31st August 1946 from a general repair, the engine changed from 5507 to 2661 on 21st October 1946 at Neasden shed, a local painter doing the job in 9in. numbers.

(below) Whilst 5509 became 2663 at Immingham shed on Sunday 13th October 1946, it had a general repair, 29th March to 3rd May 1947, from which it was out with 12in. shaded transfers for both numbers and letters. Immingham shed, June 1947.

No D11 got the BR Regional E prefix but 62664 (3rd April 1948) and 62668 (15th May 1948) got 12in. painted numbers in Gill sans but with the modified 6. When 62665 did so on 12th June 1948, it was also fitted with a cast numberplate on the smokebox, also showing the modified 6. New Holland pier.

(below) When 62661 was out on 31st December 1948, the cab side numbering was in correct Gill sans with numbers and letters matching at 10in. high. But the smokebox plates were still cast with modified 6 and 9 through to August 1949. Six got this type: 62665 (12th June 1948), 62661 (31st December 1948), 62669 (26th February 1949), 62670 (23rd April 1949), 62662 (21st May 1949) and 62663 (13th August 1949). Trafford Park shed.

In September 1949 the first British Railways emblem superseded the lettering on the tender and Gorton also corrected the 6 on the smokebox plate to Gill sans. The five which got correct plates were: 62666 (24th September 1949), 62660 (1st October 1949), 62667 (22nd October 1949), 62664 (29th April 1950) and 62668 (3rd June 1950).

Beginning with 62669, out on 3rd May 1952, this class began to acquire BR standard red, cream and grey lining. When 62668 got it on 14th May 1955 it is believed all the eleven had been so treated. Trafford Park shed, June 1953.

When 62662 had its last general repair from 17th August to 14th September 1957, it received unusual treatment in two respects. Not only was the lining retained but the tender got the smaller version of the 1949 emblem, the only one to do so. None of the class got the revised emblem of 1957. Bridlington.

Starting with 62663 on 6th October 1956, lining was again discarded and, apart from 62662, the other four to get heavy repairs later also lost their lining, these were 62667 (1st December 1956), 62670 (16th February 1957), 62666 (30th March 1957) and 62660 (17th August 1957). Staveley, May 1959.

In their final years the class was very neglected and spent considerable time out of service. This line was at Sheffield Darnall shed in May 1959. Note the GC cast plate "Not to be moved engine disabled", and the wide oval buffer heads.

Much the same position obtained in this May 1960 picture at Darnall shed. One D11 had gone in 1959 and the other ten were withdrawn between May and December 1960. Note the flattened dome cover.

No.62665 was the first to be
withdrawn, on 8th May 1959. Note
the length of the brass angle
integral with the name part. 62665
was cut up at Gorton, 62663 at
Stratford and the others went to
Doncaster to be scrapped. Gorton
works, May 1959.

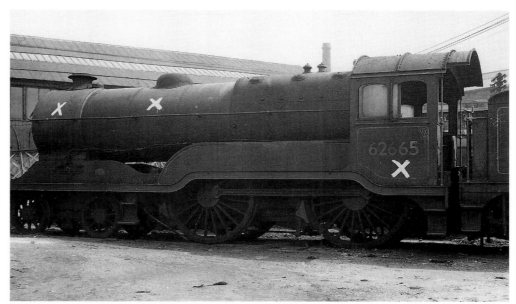

The first of the class, No.506 was
restored to original appearance for
preservation but a mistake was
made in the size of tender lettering.
This was made 7¹/₂in whereas it
should have been 6in. deep. The
front buffer beam number is also
wrong being in LNER style at 4¹/₂in.
GCR figures were 5in. and thicker
(see page 9). This photograph was
taken at Gorton works yard on 24th
September 1961, the day that
No.506 was taken over by British
Transport Commission curator of
historical relics.

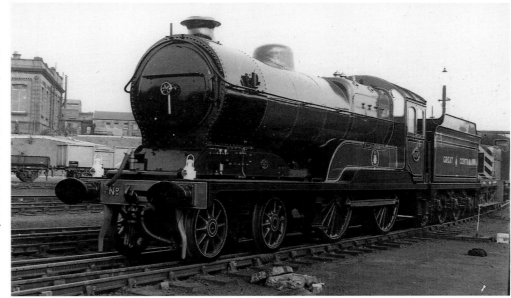

No.506 was then put on display in
the Transport Museum at
Clapham, where it stood until those
exhibits were dispersed early in
1975. It as then put in the care of
the Main Line Steam Trust at
Loughborough where (by road, on
a low loader) it arrived on 19th
March 1975. The preservation
society named Great Central
Railway operating between
Loughborough and Rothley put 506
back into working order and on
27th March 1982 it made its first
run on that stretch where it
originally worked.

Withdrawal of the D12's began in 1919 but at 1st January 1923 twelve remained to become LNER stock. All had been put into duplicate stock during 1912 to 1914 when letter B was added to their number. Those taken over were Nos. 423, 425, 428, 430, 434, 439, 440, 441, 442, 443, 446 and 128B.

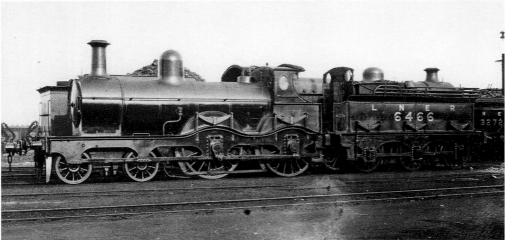

(centre) In February 1924, when the LNER numbering scheme was introduced, there were seven survivors and these were allotted numbers 6460, 6463, 6464, 6465, 6466, 6467 and 6468. Nos.6463, 6465 and 6468 were not used due to withdrawal of Nos.443B, 439B and 425B but in May 1925 No.430B became 6466 and the other three had been done at their shed by February 1925. No.6466 was an exception in having twin handles for the smokebox door fastening, the others having a wheel and handle.

(below) One of the detailed changes brought about to the class was to the buffers where, on some, the parallel shank type with collar, replaced the taper shank type fitted originally.

CLASS D 12

128B/6460

Gorton.

To traffic 7/1880.

REPAIRS:
Gor. 21/7/17—25/5/18.**G.**
Gor. 14/8—25/9/20.**G.**
Gor. 16/1/26. *Not repaired.*

BOILER:
1741.

SHED:
New Holland.

RENUMBERED:
6460 *by 9/2/25.*

CONDEMNED: 1/2/26.
Cut up at Gorton.

423B

Gorton.

To traffic 5/1877.

REPAIRS:
Gor. 12/8—16/9/16.**G.**
Gor. 20/11—18/12/20.**G.**

BOILER:
1050.

SHED:
Brunswick.

CONDEMNED: 17/5/23.
Into Gor. for cut up 20/5/23.

425B/(6468)

Gorton.

To traffic 6/1877.

REPAIRS:
Gor. 4/11/16—6/1/17.**G.**
Gor. 13/12/19—7/2/20.**G.**
Gor. 21/1—18/3/22.**G.**
Gor. 27/6/25. *Not repaired..*
Loan to GNSR. 3/6/20—19/1/21.

BOILER:
983.

SHED:
Gorton.

RENUMBERED:
6468 *allocated.*

CONDEMNED: 9/7/25.
Cut up at Gorton.

428B/6467

Gorton.

To traffic 8/1877.

REPAIRS:
Gor. 24/4—11/12/15.**G.**
Gor. 16/8—18/10/19.**G.**
Gor. 28/10—2/12/22.**G.**
Gor. 13/2/26. *Not repaired.*
Loan to GNSR. 3/6/20-19/1/21.

BOILER:
1591.

SHED:
Annesley.

RENUMBERED:
6467 *by 9/2/25.*

CONDEMNED: 1/3/26.
Cut up at Gorton.

430B/6466.

Gorton.

To traffic 9/1877.

REPAIRS:
Gor. 9/9—21/10/16.**G.**
Gor. 26/3—30/4/21.**G.**
Gor. 17/1—23/5/25.**G.**
Gor. 2/10/26. *Not repaired.*

BOILER:
149.

SHEDS:
Brunswick.
Annesley 2/6/25.
RENUMBERED:
6466 23/5/25.

CONDEMNED: 8/10/26.
Cut up at Gorton.

434B

Gorton.

To traffic 12/1877.

REPAIRS:
Gor. 21/10—23/12/16.**G.**
Gor. 7/2—13/3/20.**G.**

BOILER:
566.

SHED:
Gorton.

CONDEMNED: 13/1/23.
Cut up at Gorton.

439B/(6465)

Gorton.

To traffic 5/1878.

REPAIRS:
Gor. 5/5—10/11/17.**G.**
Gor. 11/12/20—15/1/21.**G.**
Gor. 26/9/25. *Not repaired.*

BOILER:
1090.

SHEDS:
New Holland *by 4/22.*
Annesley ?/?/?

RENUMBERED:
6465 *allocated.*

CONDEMNED: 19/10/25.
Cut up at Gorton.

440B

Gorton.

To traffic 6/1878.
REPAIRS:
Gor. 20/1—24/3/17.**G.**
Gor. 24/1—8/5/20.**G.**

BOILER:
565.

SHED:
Staveley.

CONDEMNED: 17/5/23.

Cut up at Gorton.

441B

Gorton.

To traffic 7/1878.

REPAIRS:
Gor. 15/1—12/2/16.**G.**
Gor. 14/2—27/3/20.**G.**
Gor. 11/2—25/3/22.**G.**
Gor. 9/1/23. *Not repaired.*

BOILER:
758.

SHED:
Trafford Park.

CONDEMNED: 9/1/23.
Cut up at Gorton.

442B/6464

Gorton.

To traffic 10/1878.

REPAIRS:
Gor. 30/6/17—18/5/18.**G.**
Gor. 10/12/21—21/1/22.**G.**
Gor. 11/3/30. *Not repaired.*
Loan to GNSR. 3/6/20—19/1/21.

BOILER:
1740.

SHED:
Annesley.

RENUMBERED:
6464 *by 2/25.*

CONDEMNED: 11/3/30.
Cut up at Gorton.

443B/(6463)

Gorton.

To traffic 11/1878.

REPAIRS:
Gor. 30/6—15/9/17.**G.**
Gor. 20/11/20—1/1/21.**G.**
Gor. 24/1/25. *Not repaired.*

6463 cont./
BOILER:
1585.

SHED:
Annesley.

RENUMBERED:
6463 allocated.

CONDEMNED: 26/2/25.
Cut up at Gorton.

_____

446B

Gorton.

To traffic 6/1879.

REPAIRS:
Gor. 10/4—22/5/15.**G**.
Gor. 18/8—17/11/17.**G**.
Gor. 21/8—9/10/20.**G**.

BOILER:
485.

SHED:
Brunswick.

CONDEMNED: 23/4/23.
Into Gor. for cut up 24/4/23.

_____

This buffer change was not completed as No.439ʙ kept the taper shank type on both engine and tender to withdrawal, as did 6464 and 6466. Annesley, July 1923.

The whistle position could also vary. Most had it mounted at the side of the safety valves but No.439ʙ (*see* previous view) had it on the cab roof. No.443ʙ had a buffer change at the front but not at the tender end. Annesley, July 1923.

(below) **In LNER days most of their work was on short distance local trains with a lot of it tender first running, so quite a substantial weatherboard was fitted on the tender. Note that 6464, which outlived the rest by 3¹/₂ years, practically lost its shed-applied painting and numbering and almost reverted to its Great Central livery and number. Its last general repair was in January 1922 but it worked until March 1930. Of the four which survived long enough to be renumbered, three were condemned in 1926, Nos.6466 and 6467 from Annesley and 6460 from New Holland. No.6464 continued working the Dido workmen's trains from Annesley shed until withdrawn on 11th March 1930. Immingham, 1924.**